I0796440

ADÁN MEDRANO, SERIES EDITOR

THE TEXAS MEXICAN PLANT-BASED COOKBOOK

ADÁN MEDRANO

TEXAS TECH UNIVERSITY PRESS

This book is typeset in Adobe Caslon Pro. The paper used in this book meets the minimum requirements of ANSI/NISO Z39.48-1992 (R1997). ♾

Designed by Hannah Gaskamp
Cover photograph/illustration by JoMando Cruz
Interior photography by JoMando Cruz except where otherwise specified

Library of Congress Cataloging-in-Publication Data

Names: Medrano, Adán author. Title: The Texas Mexican Plant-based Cookbook / Adán Medrano.
Description: Lubbock, Texas, USA: Texas Tech University Press, [2025] | Series: Indigenous Foodways of Texas and Northern Mexico | Includes bibliographical references and index. | Summary: "A cookbook celebrating the plant-based cuisine of Indigenous Texas Mexican communities"—Provided by publisher.
Identifiers: LCCN 2025017843 | ISBN 978-1-68283-273-8 cloth
Subjects: LCSH: Mexican American cooking | Vegan cooking | Cooking, American—Southern style | Cooking—Texas | LCGFT: Cookbooks
Classification: LCC TX715.2.S69 M468 2025 |
DDC 641.5/636209721—dc23/eng/20250416
LC record available at https://lccn.loc.gov/2025017843

Printed in China
25 26 27 28 29 30 31 32 33 / 9 8 7 6 5 4 3 2 1

Texas Tech University Press
Box 41037
Lubbock, Texas 79409-1037 USA
800.832.4042
ttup@ttu.edu
www.ttupress.org

For Richard Jiménez, my husband and creative companion.

CONTENTS

INTRODUCTION: PLANT-BASED COOKING IN THE TEXAS MEXICAN CULINARY REGION / 3

CHAPTER 1: ENCHILADAS, TAMALES, TACOS, MOLES / 13

Enchiladas Mineras 14
Enchiladas Potosinas 16
Spinach Enchiladas 18
King Trumpet Mushroom and Calabacita Green Enchiladas 20
Enfrijoladas 23
Entomatadas 24
Tamales de Hongos | Mushroom Tamales 26
Tamales de Habas y Rajas de Chiles Poblanos 28
Mesquitamal 30
Tostadas 32
Tostadas de Berenjena 35
Tacos de Hongos | Mushroom Tacos 36
Tortitas de Papa with Salsa and Salad 38
Chile con Jackfruit 40
Pipián Ranchero with Jerusalem Artichokes (Sunchokes) 42
Pipián Verde with Yucca and Calabacitas 44
Acorn Squash with Mole 46
Mole de Nuez y Mezquite | Pecan and Mesquite Mole 48

CHAPTER 2: FILETES, TORTAS, GORDITAS, TOSTADAS / 51

Cabbage and Potato Gorditas 52
Cauliflower Filets with Parsley Salsa 55
Herbed Corn and Jerusalem Artichoke Tart 56
Hibiscus Flower Drowned Torta 58
Milanesa de Zucchini con Salsa de Rábano | Zucchini Cutlets with Radish Salsa 60
Memelas Oaxaqueñas 62

CHAPTER 3: SOUPS AND SALADS / 65

Ajoblanco | Chilled Garlic Soup 67
Cold Mango Soup 68
Garbanzo and Calabacita Soup with Chipotle 71

Green Corn Soup 72
Posole Rojo 74
Posole Verde with Mushrooms 76
Sopa de Calabacitas 78
Sopa de Elote 81
Sopa Tarasca 82
Avocado and Kidney Bean Salad | Ensalada de Aguacate con Frijol 85
Cactus and Bean Salad | Ensalada de Nopalitos con Frijoles 86
Nopalitos Asados con Vinagreta al Guajillo 88
Botana de Xoconostles 91
Ensalada de Calabacita 92
Ensalada de Calabacita y Ejote 95
Ensalada de Garbanzos y Calabacitas 96
Leeks in Tomatillo Salsa 98
Kale and Red Jalapeño Salad 101
Pickled Watermelon Rind and Bean Salad 102
Watermelon and Jícama Salad with Cilantro Dressing 105

CHAPTER 4: BEANS, LENTILS, GARBANZOS / 107

Butter Beans with Poblano Rajas 109
Garbanzo, Mushroom, and Red Chile Dip 110
Lentejas Guisadas 113
Lentils with Swiss Chard | Lentejas y Acelga 114
Toksel 115

CHAPTER 5: GUISADOS Y SALTEADOS | STEWS AND SAUTÉES / 117

Calabacita Salteada 119
Calabacitas con Achiote 120
Sautéed Chayote 123
Chiles Toreados 124
Colache de Calabacitas 127
Flor de Jamaica en Chile Colorado 128
Tupinambo Salteado |Sautéed Jerusalem Artichokes 131
Mushrooms with Calabacita and Corn 132
Nopalitos with Red Chile 134
Turnip and Amaranth in Tomatillo Sauce 136
Mashed Turnip with Poblano Rajas 138

CHAPTER 6: RICE AND PASTA / 141

Chile Poblano Rice 143
Conchitas | Shell Pasta 144
Mushroom and Green Olive Rice 147
Mushroom Paella 148

CHAPTER 7: CONDIMENTS / 151

Chile Dulce | Bell Pepper Salsa 152
Cebollas Encurtidas 153
Chamoy Casero 155
Nopal Pico de Gallo 156

Cashew Crumble 158
Queso de Almendras 159
Chile Ancho en Escabeche 160
Chile Sal 161
Chile Serrano Vinaigrette 163
Crema de Cajú (Anacardo / Nuez de la India) | Cashew Cream 164
Jícama Cranberry Conserve 166
Mojo de Ajo 167
Chile Piquín Salsa 168
Serrano Crudo Salsa 169
Brown Vegetable Stock 171
White Vegetable Stock 172

CHAPTER 8: BEVERAGES / 175

Bajicopo 177
Cranberry Rosemary Champagne Cocktail 178
Mesquite Agua Fresca 180
Tepache 183
Yaupon Holly Tea 184

CHAPTER 9: SWEETS / 187

Avocado Popsicle | Paleta de Aguacate 189
Atole de Mesquite | Mesquite Porridge 190
Nicuatole 193
Pecan Blueberry Chia Pudding 194
Quinoa Pancakes 197

CONCLUSION: A PARTNERSHIP WITH THE PLANT COMMUNITY / 199

LIST OF RECIPES / 203

REFERENCES / 205

INDEX / 211

THE TEXAS MEXICAN PLANT-BASED COOKBOOK

WITH PHOTOGRAPHY
BY JOMANDO CRUZ

INTRODUCTION

PLANT-BASED COOKING IN THE TEXAS MEXICAN CULINARY REGION

This book is about the plant-based traditions and recipes of my ancestors, the first people to inhabit what is now Texas and Northeastern Mexico over 15,000 years ago. They are the Coahuiltecan, Caddo, Atakapa-Ishak, Akokisa, Karankawa, Tonkawa, and hundreds of other Native peoples who hunted, gathered, and cooked across a vast landscape that extends from Austin, Texas, to Monterrey, Mexico. They mastered cooking with fire and developed innovative techniques like the earth oven, the precursor to today's wood-burning ovens and modern electric or gas ovens.

Interestingly, earth ovens were predominantly used to cook plants. One of the latter was sotol (*Dasylirion texanum*), which is used today to yield the alcoholic drink of the same name. The sotol bulb was a food staple that our ancestors slow-cooked in earth ovens. Cooking sotol bulbs for 36–48 hours breaks down indigestible long-chain carbohydrates and poisonous compounds and renders them edible, nutritious, and delicious, tasting like nutty molasses syrup ("Sotol," n.d.).

This type of knowledge about the nutrition and flavor of plants is a rich culinary heritage that deserves greater recognition. It is an important part of the history of Indigenous Mexican American people who live and cook in this part of the world. Plants continue to be essential to a sustainable diet that in many instances includes meat. But just as important as providing excellent nutrition, plants can also open up and connect us to the beauty of Mother Earth, even as they did for our ancestors.

Early Native peoples easily moved from the Nueces River in Texas to the Sabinas River in Coahuila and the Rio Grande in between. I call this landscape the Texas Mexican region, and it includes the Mexican northeastern states that border Texas: Tamaulipas, Nuevo León, Coahuila, and Chihuahua. The area is also called the Coahuiltecan region, the name deriving from the Mexican state of Coahuila. People in this region share a common history and culture. They also share the same cuisine, because over thousands of years these varied groups interacted with each other, developing hunting techniques, using the same ingredients from the land, and inventing a variety of cooking technologies.

Over millennia, the repertoire of these early home cooks expanded from fire roasting and boiling to include baking in earth ovens, steaming, drying, smoking, stewing, and roasting. They utilized mortars to grind mesquite pods and nuts, preparing dishes with squash, corn, and beans. In fact, families who lived here in the distant past gave us many of the flavors and cooking techniques that we enjoy today, even though we may not be aware that they are a Native American heritage.

The cooking practices were remarkably consistent throughout the region as well (Thoms, n.d.), with shared tools and methods shaping the culinary landscape. Among these are bedrock mortars, found scattered across the terrain today. Some are deep holes extending an arm's length, while others are shallow and bowl-shaped. Early cooks relied on these mortars to grind mesquite, seeds, and nuts, which they mixed with dried meat to create pemmican, a nutrient-dense dried sausage. They also crushed the pink fruit of the cactus and mashed sweet mesquite pods to make early versions of agua fresca drinks.

Stone-boiling was another common method used to prepare soups and stews. Cooks would dig a large hole in the ground, resembling a pot, line it with leather or bark, and fill it with liquid. Heated stones were then added to bring the contents to a simmer or boil, depending on the dish being prepared. Many of the cooking techniques we use today—including boiling, roasting, steaming, and baking—were developed by early women and Two-Spirit cooks who infused their dishes with flavors that reflected the seasons and the terroir. Cooking, by nature, was inherently local and seasonal, a tradition that continues to shape modern cuisine.

Over time, when their lives were tragically disrupted with the arrival of conquest-minded Europeans who brought with them catastrophic diseases, Native peoples dispersed and sought safety in any space they could find. Sometimes they fled to friendly Catholic missions or to towns along the countryside that seemed safe, or they were caught and sold into slavery. They did prevail, staying together, and eventually blended and became today's Texas Mexican American community (La Vere, 2004). Cultural geographer Daniel D. Arreola uses the term Texas Mexican to describe Mexican Americans of South Texas and asserts that Texas Mexican foodways remain distinctive and particular to residents of South Texas. He writes that Texas Mexican foodways "are emblematic of the region and thereby part of the Texas Mexican identity" (Arreola, 2002, 163).

In writing this cookbook, I extend the term to include Northeastern Mexico because although in 1848 the Rio Grande became a geopolitical border that separated families, it did not erase the bonds of family and culture that for millennia shaped their food traditions. When I was growing up, my family owned land in San Antonio, Texas (140 miles north of the Rio Grande) and in Nava, Coahuila (25 miles south of the Rio Grande). We regularly traveled back and forth between our two homes. In both places, we visited with our extended family and enjoyed home-cooked meals consisting of such fare as tortillas, carne guisada, nopalitos, salsas, and guacamole.

Crossing the border did not magically change the flavor of our extended family's home cooking. The avocado taco of San Antonio tastes the same as the one in Nava. So does the flour tortilla, the serrano salsa, the barbacoa, and every other traditional dish. Texas Mexican food expresses the flavors cooked by families with ancestral roots in this larger landscape that now traverses two countries. Cuisine transcends and enriches national borders, bringing vitality and cultural connection. This happens in every part of the world.

As an analogous example, Koksijde, Belgium, is a beach resort where I worked one spring in a fine dining restaurant. In the kitchen I quickly saw the flavor similarities of Belgian cooking with the bordering neighbors, France and the Netherlands. It was not just the ingredients—like white asparagus, leeks, and endive—they shared because of their proximity. They also had in common certain techniques like deep frying and boiling down stocks. Food demonstrates that borders are actually places of shared landscapes and cultural exchange. Even when borders are walled into fortresses, plants grow and spread freely, shaped by weather and land formations, with their seeds carried by birds that soar across terrain, unhindered by immigration checkpoints or political borders.

The Gault archaeological site, north of Austin, contains remains of a large community and evidence of its cooking practices. It is over 15,000 years old. The people who lived there cooked pronghorn antelopes, turkeys, deer, rabbits, ducks, and quail, and the evidence extends to turtle bones, mollusks, and burnt frog bones. The evidence there, along with that of other sites, suggests that they also ate other familiar specialties such as pecans and black walnuts, as well as acorns, grapes, berries, seeds, and tubers. Mesquite and cactus were central to celebratory eating and sharing. It is these plant-based traditions, often overlooked, that I want to honor with this cookbook.

Among the overlooked local plant foods is cactus (nopalitos), familiar to most Texans and Mexicans as a natural and unique character in both rural and urban landscapes. The nopal is at home in farms, ranches, backyards, and parking lots. I hope more of us will discover wonderful ways to enjoy the herbaceous and tangy flavor of the young and tender paddles.

Mesquite beans or pods are another delicious food that was central to our diet 2,000 years ago, but which we've stopped eating and which I hope we will rediscover. They are sweet, with a complex and intense flavor reminiscent of chocolate or caramel. Our ancestors ground them to make beverages and purées and cooked them to make sweets and tamales. But mesquite is no longer widely used in our Mexican American kitchens and restaurants. Our food and Native American identities were erased by design.

In 1837, the Standing Committee on Indian Affairs of the Republic of Texas issued its report to then-President Sam Houston and declared: "The People called Lipan, Karankawa and Tonkawa your Committee considers as part of the Mexican nation and [are] no longer to be considered as a different People" (Winfrey & Day, 1966, 22). My ancestors, Native peoples, suddenly became Mexicans and the native character of our food was erased from the public record.

Food writers of the 1970s began defining the Mexican food of Texas as an Anglo-Texan creation. They started calling it "tex-mex," describing it as south-of-the-border food transformed by American tastes, and they completely overlooked the indigenous roots of the food. The recipes in this book will celebrate what was overlooked. This cookbook is not about Tex-Mex. Ours is not a hyphenated cuisine, nor is our community a hyphenated community.

Neither is our cuisine hegemonic or uniform. Rather, it is part of the larger Mexican cuisine that is a family of various regional cooking styles that share the same general flavor profile. Regions with different landscapes and terroirs use the same iconic ingredients like chiles, corn, mesquite, beans, and squash, as well as the same technologies and techniques like charring, drying, and oven roasting. However, each is a unique regional expression that is tied to the local flora, fauna, and migration. Some well-known regional styles are Oaxaca Mexican food, Yucatán Mexican food, and Puebla Mexican food. Texas Mexican food is not so well known.

The recipes in this book represent the comida casera, home-style cooking, of native Texas Mexican American families. Texas Mexican food is also cooked in restaurants and cafes that are located in Mexican American neighborhoods, and they number in the thousands throughout Texas. Texas Mexican restaurants hold an important historical protagonism in the US that has not been told. Their success gave rise to the well-known Tex-Mex.

Tex-Mex restaurants serve food that differs from Texas Mexican food in two ways. First, they have different flavor profiles. Among the most identifiable flavor differences are the Tex-Mex preference for deep frying as a technique over roasting, steaming, and drying; heavy use of cumin as a seasoning; and covering most dishes with a layer of melted yellow cheese. The second difference is the history of their origin.

Many pinpoint the cuisine's origins to Anglos who imitated cafes of San Antonio's Westside Mexican American neighborhoods. *Dallas Morning News* restaurant critic Leslie Brenner writes that "the genre was born of a cultural sin" (Brenner, 2020). In the late 1800s, Chicagoan Otis Farnsworth visited Westside San Antonio, saw the many neighborhood cafes, and was hugely impressed by their success. These were the same flavors and dishes that native Mexican women were selling in open-air stands in downtown San Antonio with equal success.

Later called chili queens, these chef/owners

had single-handedly turned downtown San Antonio into a culinary tourist destination and business was booming. Unfortunately, the women were increasingly harassed and eventually forced out of the city center. Recognizing the opportunity in the wake of this racist expulsion, Farnsworth decided to open one of these restaurants himself. His restaurant would not be like the open-air stands of the women. With his wife, Sarah Roach Farnsworth, he opened an expensively constructed brick and mortar restaurant in a prime downtown location. His clientele would be Anglo Texans who loved the food but would never think of frequenting Westside barrio cafes for dinner. He named it "The Original Mexican Restaurant." By Anglos, for Anglos: that's how Tex-Mex food began (Pilcher, 2012).

Such restaurants exploded in popularity. They are different from the neighborhood Texas Mexican cafes, which they imitated, in ways that speak to class, taste, cultural awareness, and indigenous memory. The dishes served in the Mexican cafes of Texas are traditional ones—like the vegetable soup, caldo; the nopalitos (cactus) with tomato and chile; and the enfrijolada, soft corn tortillas infused with a velvety bean and herb sauce—that would not be found in Tex-Mex restaurants. These dishes are plant-based, delicious, and healthy.

I'm writing this cookbook with a mix of hope and urgency. My hope is that these recipes, along with their stories, will bring more joy and pleasure to your cooking while deepening our connection to the earth beneath our feet and the sky above. But this joy is increasingly at risk. We live in a troubling time when the food we eat—and the ways we grow and prepare it—is often harming our health. It wasn't always this way.

When Europeans first arrived in the Americas in 1492 and in Texas in 1528, bent on conquest, they brought with them diseases for which the Native peoples had no immunity. Europeans infected the entire population of Texas with smallpox, measles, and cholera, leading to the deaths of ninety percent of the Native peoples of Texas between 1492 and 1900 (La Vere, 2004). These massive losses remain a painful memory and consequence of colonization. Today, we face a different but equally devastating threat—obesity, type 2 diabetes, and cardiovascular disease. Unlike infectious diseases, these modern health crises stem primarily from diet, yet they are still tied to the legacy of conquest and systemic disenfranchisement.

In 2017–2018, obesity affected 50.4 percent of Mexican Americans and 44.8 percent of Latinx individuals, compared to 42.2 percent of the non-Latinx White population (Alemán et al., 2023). This condition often leads to serious health issues, including stroke, arthritis, sleep apnea, some cancers, and premature death (CDC, 2024). Research indicates that the more disconnected Latinx individuals are from traditional foodways, the higher their risk of obesity. Those who adhere to ancestral dietary practices tend to consume healthier foods rich in fiber and low in saturated fats, whereas those who adopt mainstream American diets consume fewer starchy roots and vegetables but higher amounts of high-glycemic fruits (Yoshida et al., 2016; Vidal et al., 2022). Additionally, food insecurity exacerbates these issues. In 2020, one in three Latinx and Mexican American individuals lived in households experiencing material hardship, including food shortages (Bureau, 2022). These conditions contribute to high sugar intake and reliance on processed foods (Vidal et al., 2022).

Addressing these health crises requires reclaiming traditional foodways. Generational amnesia, where knowledge of ancestral food sourcing and preparation fades over time, must be countered with active remembrance and practice (Kahn Jr., 2002). One approach is "civic agriculture," which strengthens local food systems through home and community gardens. The University of Texas Rio Grande Valley (UTRGV) Agroecology Program exemplifies this effort with its Hub of Prosperity, a five-acre urban farm situated at the First Methodist Church in Edinburg, Texas. Collaborating with local schools and community members, the farm provides fresh produce, fosters agricultural education, and supports sustainable farming research. Similar programs nationwide are revitalizing Indigenous food traditions and reinforcing the connection between food, health, and community.

The importance of these efforts is evident in student engagement. At a UTRGV panel discussion, high school student Marcos Cano described his experience planting a salsa and butterfly garden. He and his classmates shared their harvest through cooking demonstrations, deepening their connection to the flavors of their culinary heritage and to native ingredients. "Bees keep plants alive; don't kill the bees," Cano emphasized, reflecting a broader awareness of ecological interdependence. He continued, "You have to experience seeing the small seed grow into giant, fruit-bearing plants. It's the greatest feeling. We look forward to harvest day all year" (UTRGV, n.d.). His passion for gardening illustrates how reconnecting with traditional foodways fosters both personal and communal well-being.

The triple threat of obesity, type 2 diabetes, and cardiovascular disease cannot be remedied by pointing the finger at an individual's dietary choices. Instead, social determinants of health—economic and political structures that limit access to traditional foods—play a defining role. Poverty, acculturation, and a food system designed to promote highly processed, unhealthy options all contribute to these disparities (One-on-One with a Public Health Professor, 2023). Counteracting these forces requires deliberate efforts to revive Indigenous food traditions, making them accessible and integral to daily life.

Reclaiming ancestral culinary knowledge is a journey of rediscovery. The recipes in this book highlight the Texas Mexican region's long-standing plant-based traditions, along with select contributions from other parts of Mexico that reflect centuries of regional exchange. Some recipes feature native ingredients that have fallen out of use, such as sunflower roots, yaupon holly leaves, and mesquite bean pods.

By reintroducing these flavors, we can reconnect with our heritage and develop a deeper appreciation for the natural world. This is a vision that I've learned from the tomatoes, cucumbers, and countless other plants I hoed, picked, washed, and carried. When we approach plants with respect and wonder, they can teach us how to live not as conquerors but as partners, discovering and embracing our place on this planet.

I write from the perspective of a migrant farmworker. From the day I was born until I turned sixteen, my days were spent in agricultural fields, croplands with nothing but swaying leaves, flower petals, dark earth, and gritty sand. My mom recounted how, as a toddler, I walked so cheerfully among rows of bush green beans, swathed by the pods and leaves. I remember sunny afternoons when, as a boy, I often lay on my back and smiled at the cumulus clouds shape-shifting across that beautiful blue that belongs only to the sky.

With my brothers and sisters, I've picked cotton all over Texas in cities like Robstown and Hillsboro. I hoed sugar beets and soybeans in Au Gres, Michigan, and Crookston, Minnesota. Both Texas and the US Midwest formed my sense of landscape and my understanding of plants as living beings to be eaten, but also to be respected and honored as co-inhabitants on earth.

In Des Moines, Iowa, I picked tomatoes starting at daylight and ending 10 hours later, a couple of hours before dusk. Bent over all day, I dragged a basket across acres and acres of tomato fields, filling it with red tomatoes, one row at a time, one plant at a time, one fruit at a time. We got a break on Saturdays when we stopped at noon so we could bathe and go into town to buy groceries and sightsee. Sunday was a day of rest. Migrant farmwork was grueling, monotonous, compulsory labor, and I don't remember how I was able to handle the drudgery. But from that Iowa time in my life, I do carry with me a sensation of natural joy. To know the land is a gift.

Whenever I brush across a tomato plant, the fragrance enters me and I'm back with a friend from my childhood. The distinctive, marvelous aroma that the leaves release, together with that emanating from the delicious ripe fruit, construct a bodily experience that grounds me, grounds me on a piece of earth that I'm sharing with a tomato plant.

My understanding of companionship with nature grew naturally and unexpectedly. It took root during the years I spent surrounded by endless greenery, shaped by the quiet guidance of my parents. They taught me through their actions and demeanor, showing me how to respect and nurture the world around us. Today, I love to garden, and I cherish the plants that share my home, forming a bond with them even amidst the hardships of those earlier years. To me, this enduring connection is a powerful reminder that friendship with nature is an intrinsic part of being human.

It was in another Iowa town, Muscatine, that I started becoming more aware of my physical connection to the character of dirt and to the sentient life of plants. It was also when I first realized that there were two stories to my life: one that I knew and understood, and another that was not mine and that made me angry.

I was on my knees picking cucumbers. I know the smell of freshly picked cucumbers, how to pick them from the top, careful not to touch the scratchy, irritating underside of the leaves. Being so close to them for so long leads to understanding. But that day I was suffering.

It was a cool, wet morning, the dew still dripping from the cucumber plants, making the ground muddy. It was early enough that bumblebees swarmed around the yellow flowers. I was wet, dirty, and cold, scared of getting stung again. I know in my bones what it means to be truly miserable.

Then two young boys, not Mexican American like me, walked toward me across the cucumber rows. They wore laundered, ironed clothes, their white faces and hands clean, hair well groomed, just a little mud on their shoes. They looked like the pictures of white boys I'd seen in magazines. They wanted to talk to me.

One of the boys was holding a writing pad and pencil, and they said they were taking a survey. I answered their questions about my age and hometown of San Antonio, but I can't remember what else they asked or how I answered. The one thing that I remember clearly is the image of two boys with clean clothes and clean hands standing over me, about to turn me into a set of statistics. It filled me with an anger that, surprisingly, centered me.

My story was misery in the mud and relationship with plants. Their story about me I will never know. But I knew then that it was wrong for them to stand over me. One way or another I would tell my story about working with plants in the fields.

That encounter transformed me into an inquisitive and driven learner. From that experience I am able to pursue the questions about food that need answers, the type of answers that can lead to change. Why is there systemic poverty that privileges white people and takes away opportunity from Mexican Americans?

What does it take to make change, real change, and what part can I play in that process?

This cookbook is an invitation to embrace plant-based cooking as both a culinary and cultural revival. These traditions offer nutrient-rich, low-fat, and low-calorie food sources that complement our broader culinary history. More importantly, they provide a pathway to better health—not only for the half of our community suffering from obesity but for all of us. Beyond physical well-being, reclaiming these foodways strengthens cultural identity and fosters resilience.

Through the recipes and stories in this book, I aim to deepen our connection to the earth and to each other. Plant-based traditions stand alongside animal-based food practices as vital components of our culinary heritage. By reclaiming these foodways, we honor our ancestors, empower our communities, and shape a healthier, more sustainable future.

GreenPoint
www.greenpointdist.com

CHAPTER 1

ENCHILADAS, TAMALES, TACOS, MOLES

ENCHILADAS MINERAS

This dish is from Guanajuato, in the Mexican state of the same name, and it is called miner's enchiladas because of the silver mines there. It's a nutritious, vegetable-laden dish that women prepared for the miners, who were male.

Beginning in 1548, when Spaniards discovered silver, Guanajuato grew in importance, and by the mid-eighteenth-century Guanajuato became the leading producer of silver in the world. That status was achieved largely on the backs of Indigenous peoples of Mexico who worked the mines. Fernando Serrano conducted an in-depth study of the working conditions of the Indigenous mine workers in the states of Guanajuato and Michoacán. He describes the impact on communities of the mining institutions, including a forced labor draft (Serrano, 2017).

Interestingly, this is a dish that gives me pleasure but also links to sad aspects of the suffering of native peoples. Food works that way, connecting us to our past while nourishing us.

INGREDIENTS (SERVES 4)

- 8 guajillo chiles
- 1 clove garlic
- 1/2 tsp. cumin seeds
- 1/2 tsp. dried oregano
- 1 Tbs. canola or vegetable oil
- 12 corn tortillas
- 1 small white onion, diced
- 1 romaine lettuce, sliced
- 12 oz. carrots, diced
- 10 oz. potatoes, diced
- 1/4 cup sliced pickled jalapeños
- 1/2 cup queso de almendras (p. 159) (optional)

METHOD

1. Deseed and devein the chiles and roast them on a hot comal (griddle) for a few seconds until they start to change color. Place them in a saucepan, cover them with water, and bring to a boil. Turn off the heat and let the chiles soak for 15 minutes.
2. Peel and dice the carrots; place them in a pot of boiling water and cook for 5 minutes or untill they are tender when pierced but not mushy. Drain and set aside.
3. Peel and dice the potatoes; place them in a pot of boiling water and cook for 5 minutes or until they are tender when pierced but not mushy. Drain and set aside.
4. Heat a small pan over medium heat, then add the cumin and oregano and toss or stir for about 3–4 minutes until they become fragrant. Transfer to a cool plate and set aside.
5. In a blender, add the rehydrated chiles, garlic, toasted cumin, and oregano and blend on high to make a smooth, velvety purée. Add 1/4 cup water if needed to blend. There should not be any granules or particles, but if there are, sift through a fine mesh sieve.
6. Heat 1 Tbs. canola or vegetable oil in a Dutch oven and add the chile purée. Cook for 5–8 minutes. The color will deepen and the purée will thicken.
7. Using tongs or spatulas, dip each tortilla in the chile for 6–8 seconds so that the tortilla soaks up the chile. Transfer to a plate, lying flat, and add 1 tsp. diced onion.

Roll it and proceed in the same way with the other tortillas, keeping them warm. Before serving, the plates of enchiladas can be heated in the microwave for 20 seconds.

8. Garnish the enchiladas, 3 per plate, with the sliced lettuce, carrots, potatoes, and pickled jalapeño slices. Top with queso de almendras (p. 159) if desired.

These enchiladas make a colorful, gleeful presentation.

ENCHILADAS POTOSINAS

These enchiladas may look like an empanada or a quesadilla, but they are truly enchiladas because the corn masa is infused with chile. That is what enchilada means: a tortilla infused with chile. I've adapted the recipe that was created in the mid-1800s in the small town of Soledad de Graciano Sánchez, which is within the larger metropolitan area of San Luis Potosí. Credit for the recipe is given to Cristina Jalomo (Zaragoza, 2022).

I include this recipe for two reasons. First, it demonstrates how you can have a dry enchilada simply by infusing the masa with chile and then making a tortilla. Second, my great-grandfather was from a town just 90 miles north of San Luis Potosí. I'm reminded that for centuries the ancestors of Texas Mexican American families regularly traveled throughout what is now North and Central Mexico. I celebrate our ancestral connections that have led to the traditions of sharing recipes and cooking techniques.

INGREDIENTS (SERVES 4)

- 3 chiles anchos, stems removed
- 2 cups masa harina (finely ground corn flour, not corn meal)
- 2 cups water
- 2 cloves garlic, minced
- 2 Roma tomatoes, diced
- 1 chile serrano, minced
- 1 Tbs. vegetable oil
- 1/4 cup vegetable oil to brush on the enchiladas
- 1 small white onion, sliced into thin rounds
- 1 avocado, sliced
- salt to taste
- 1/2 cup crema de cajú (p. 164) (optional)

METHOD

Preheat oven to 400°F

1. On a comal (griddle), medium heat, roast the chiles anchos until they form some black spots.
2. In a saucepan, place the chiles and cover them with water. Bring to a boil, then turn off the heat and hydrate the chiles for 15 minutes.
3. Place the chiles in a blender with 1/2 cup of water and blend on high until the purée is smooth and velvety. There should not be any small particles, but if there are some, strain through a fine mesh sieve.
4. In a bowl, place the masa harina and add the chile ancho purée plus the additional 1 1/2 cups of water. Combine well, then cover with a dry cloth and let stand for 20 minutes for the corn to rehydrate.
5. In a skillet, heat the vegetable oil over medium heat. Add the tomatoes, garlic, and chile serrano and cook for 5 minutes. Add salt to taste. Set aside.
6. Make 12 small balls from the chile ancho masa and press them using a tortilla press covered with plastic wrap to keep the masa from sticking. Cook the tortillas on a comal (griddle), medium heat, so that they are partially cooked on both sides.
7. When the tortillas are partially cooked, place some of the tomato mixture on one half, then fold and crimp the edges with your fingers as if making an empanada or turnover.

8. To finish cooking, brush the empanada-like enchiladas with vegetable oil, place on a cookie sheet, and bake for 5–7 minutes so that they deepen in color.

Serve immediately garnished with the avocado slices and the onion rounds.

Optional: Spoon some crema de cajú (p. 164) over the enchiladas.

SPINACH ENCHILADAS

Spinach enchiladas are common in many Texas Mexican restaurants, served as a vegetarian dish, although we never ate them in our home when I was growing up. Spinach is related to beets and Swiss chard. It was first cultivated in Iran over 2,000 years ago, was taken to Spain by the Arabs during their 800-year occupation of the Iberian Peninsula, and reached us after conquest (Mahr, n.d.).

With raisins and pine nuts, this is a tasty party dish, made extra special with a topping of fresh salsa ranchera.

INGREDIENTS (SERVES 4)

- 3 pasilla chiles
- 3/4 cup water
- additional water as needed
- 12 corn tortillas
- 1 Tbs. canola oil
- 1/4 cup cilantro, coarsely chopped

FOR THE SALSA RANCHERA

- 2 lbs. Roma tomatoes
- 4 oz. quartered white onion
- 2 serrano chiles (use only 1 chile for a less hot salsa)
- 2 cloves garlic, unpeeled
- 1 1/2 tsp. salt or to taste

FOR THE SPINACH MIXTURE

- 2 lbs. fresh spinach
- 2 Tbs. canola oil
- 6 Tbs. pine nuts
- 6 Tbs. dark raisins
- 1/2 tsp. salt or to taste

METHOD

1. Slice open the pasilla chiles and remove the stem, the seeds, and the veins. Place them in a saucepan and cover them with water. Cover the pan and bring the water to a boil. Then turn off the heat and let the chiles rehydrate for 20 minutes, until soft and pliable.
2. Place the chiles in a blender with 3/4 cup water and blend on high until they form a smooth purée with no granules. You may have to let the chiles cool before doing this, depending on your blender. If there are still some particles, strain through a fine mesh sieve.
3. Heat 1 Tbs. canola oil in a large saucepan, then pour in the chile purée. Watch for splatter, keeping a lid handy to cover the saucepan halfway as necessary. Fry the chile for about 6 minutes until the color deepens. Add just enough water so that the chile is slightly soupy and thinly covers the back of a spoon. Set aside and keep warm.

TO MAKE THE SALSA RANCHERA

1. In a comal (griddle) or cast iron skillet, roast the tomatoes, onion, serrano chiles, and garlic cloves until they roast and develop black spots, about 7 minutes.
2. Unpeel the garlic cloves and place them with the serrano chiles and one half of the tomatoes in a blender and blend for a few seconds until smooth. Add the onion and the remaining tomatoes and blend for 4 to 7 seconds, just enough to incorporate the

onion and the tomato but still have some tiny bits of texture. Add salt to taste. Set aside and keep warm.

TO MAKE THE SPINACH MIXTURE

1. Cook the spinach in boiling water for about 3 minutes. Drain and allow to cool. When it is cool enough to handle, squeeze clumps of spinach very tightly to remove all the moisture. Chop the spinach into small pieces, then separate the clumps.
2. In a large skillet, heat 2 Tbs. canola oil and add the spinach, raisins, pine nuts, and salt. Stir vigorously to separate any spinach clumps and incorporate the raisins and pine nuts. Cook for 2–5 minutes until the pine nuts begin to brown. Set aside and keep warm.

TO ASSEMBLE THE ENCHILADAS

Working with two spatulas, dip a corn tortilla into the warm pasilla chile for about 5 seconds. Depending on how dry your tortillas are, it may take 8 seconds, but watch carefully because if you dip them for too long, they will fall apart. Remove the chile-infused tortilla and place it on a plate. Add 3 Tbs. of the spinach mixture and roll it, seam side down. Do this with all of the tortillas, transferring them 3 to each serving plate. Spoon 1 Tbs. of salsa ranchera over each enchilada and serve immediately. Place the remaining salsa in a bowl for guests who may want additional salsa. As necessary, reheat the enchilada plates for 5 minutes in a 350°F oven or in a microwave oven for 30 seconds.

Garnish with the fresh chopped cilantro.

KING TRUMPET MUSHROOM AND CALABACITA GREEN ENCHILADAS

Green enchiladas take a big leap into chile territory in this recipe because they are infused with both poblano and serrano chiles. An enchilada is basically a "chilified" tortilla. In other green enchilada recipes they are most often infused with a green tomatillo-based chile sauce.

These poblano-serrano flavored tortillas are jam-packed with a combination of three toothsome ingredients: king trumpet mushrooms, calabacitas, and hominy. The finishing sauce couples the standard tomatillos with pepitas (pumpkin seeds), so you'll taste a semblance to pipián. I think this is a celebratory dinner dish.

INGREDIENTS (MAKES 12 ENCHILADAS)

- 4 oz. king trumpet mushrooms
- 1 yellow squash, 9 oz.
- 2 Tbs. extra virgin olive oil
- 4 oz. hominy
- 3 poblano chiles
- 1 serrano chile, 4 inches long
- 2 cups water
- 1 tsp. salt
- 12 corn tortillas

FOR THE SAUCE

- 12 oz. tomatillos
- 1/2 cup pepitas (pumpkin seeds), roasted
- 2 cloves garlic
- 2 Tbs. minced parsley
- 1 chile de árbol
- 1/2 tsp. Mexican oregano
- 1/2 tsp. salt
- 1/4 cup water
- 1 white onion, sliced into 1/8-inch-thick half-rings
- 1 large leaf of epazote (optional)

METHOD

1. Place the poblano chiles under a broiler and cook until the skin blisters and chars, turning them as needed. Make sure they don't burn. Remove them from the oven and cover with a damp cloth for 15 minutes. When they are cool enough to handle, cut a slit along one side and remove the stem and all the seeds and white membranes. Set aside.
2. Place the tomatillos (hulled and washed) and the serrano chile in a saucepan, cover with water, and bring to a boil. Cover them, lower the heat, and cook for 15 minutes, until their bright green color changes. Drain and set aside.

3. Wash any dirt off the trumpet mushrooms and slice them carefully lengthwise into 1/4-inch strips, then cut them in 1/2-inch little sticks. Set aside.
4. Wash the yellow squash, then cut it into 1-inch dice. Set aside.
5. In a blender, place the boiled chile serrano and the poblano chiles, 1 tsp. salt, and 2 cups of water. Blend on high until the ingredients are completely smooth. Transfer to a skillet and hold warm on very low heat.
6. In a blender, place the tomatillos, pepitas, garlic, chile de árbol, oregano, parsley, epazote (if using), 1/2 tsp. salt, and 1/4 cup of water. Blend on high until the ingredients form a perfectly smooth purée. It may take up to 2 minutes or slightly longer for the pumpkin seeds to liquify. Set aside.
7. In a 12-inch skillet, heat 2 Tbs. extra virgin olive oil until the surface becomes wavy. Add the mushrooms and squash and sauté for 7 minutes, until they are cooked, stirring as needed. Add the hominy, cover, lower the heat, and cook for 2 minutes. Uncover and add about 1/4 cup of water to deglaze the skillet. Set aside.
8. To assemble the enchiladas, place a large plate next to the skillet with the poblano and serrano chiles. Using two spatulas, dip a tortilla in the warm chile sauce for about 8 seconds to infuse it with the chiles. Be mindful that if you leave it too long, the tortilla may fall apart. Lift from the skillet and place it on the plate, then add 3 Tbs. of the mushroom mixture. Roll the tortilla and place on serving plates (3 per plate) or batch them onto a platter, seam side down. Do this with all of the tortillas. If you have a lot of the poblano-serrano sauce left, spoon some over the enchiladas. Finally, spoon 1 1/2 Tbs. of the tomatillo purée over each of the enchiladas. You may reheat either the plates or the platter in a 350°F oven for 10 minutes.

Garnish with the onion slices and serve immediately.

ENFRIJOLADAS

Enfrijoladas are like enchiladas, and it's all about infusing corn tortillas with a flavorsome sauce. The adjective, enchilada, is the past participle of the verb *enchilar*, which means to infuse with chile. So, a tortilla enchilada means a tortilla that's infused with chile.

By the same token, a tortilla enfrijolada means a tortilla that's infused with beans (*frijoles*). This recipe infuses corn tortillas with a delicate sauce that uses pinto beans as the base. Enfrijoladas are a delicious tradition, and highly nutritious, because when beans are combined with corn, they become a complete protein (Staff, 2011).

INGREDIENTS (MAKES 12 ENFRIJOLADAS)

- 2 cups cooked pinto beans
- 1 small clove garlic
- 1/4 cup white onion, diced
- 1 Tbs. canola or vegetable oil
- 1/4 tsp. black peppercorns
- 1 whole allspice
- 1 dried chipotle chile, deseeded, deveined
- 1 1/2 cups water (for rehydrating chile)
- 2 tsp. white distilled vinegar
- 1/8 tsp. thyme
- 3/4 tsp. salt
- 1 1/2 cups brown vegetable broth
- Thin slices of white onion for garnish
- 12 corn tortillas
- queso de almendras (optional) (p. 159)
- 1/2 cup crema de cajú (optional) (p. 164)

METHOD

1. Place deseeded and deveined chipotle chile in a saucepan with 1 1/2 cups water and bring to a boil. Turn off the heat and let the chile rehydrate for 15 minutes until they are soft and pliable.
2. In a small skillet, sauté the onion in 1 Tbs. canola or vegetable oil for about 5 minutes until translucent and soft.
3. In a blender, place the chile chipotle, onion, and all the other ingredients, including the brown vegetable broth, and blend on high to make a very smooth, velvety purée.
4. In a large saucepan or Dutch oven, place the bean purée and bring to a boil. Lower the heat and simmer for 30 minutes so that the flavors develop and the sauce thickens.

TO MAKE THE ENFRIJOLADAS

1. Dip each tortilla in a bowl of water, then immediately place it on a comal (griddle) at 350°F. Heat the tortilla for about 2 minutes, then turn to heat the other side. The tortillas should develop golden and black roasted spots.
2. Using a couple of spatulas, immerse the tortilla in the bean sauce for about 5–6 seconds to infuse it with the sauce. Transfer to a plate and fold the tortilla in half. Place 3 folded tortillas enfrijoladas on each plate, then spoon on some extra bean sauce. Garnish with the sliced onion and, if desired, sprinkle with queso de almendras (p. 159) or top with crema de cajú (p. 164).

ENTOMATADAS

Like enfrijoladas and enchiladas, entomatadas feature deliciously made corn tortillas that have been infused with a carefully blended sauce. Enchiladas are infused with a chile-based sauce, enfrijoladas are infused with a bean-based sauce, and these entomatadas are infused with a tomate-based sauce. Don't add chiles to this sauce because then they would become enchiladas instead of entomatadas.

Both the French and the Italians are famous for having versions of the original Mexican entomatada sauce. The French declare that their tomato sauce is one of the six mother sauces of French cuisine, and they use the same basic ingredients of these entomatadas: tomatoes, onion, and garlic. The Italian tomato sauce, marinara, pairs beautifully with their famous pastas. But these lush corn tortillas entomatadas are the original pairing of Mexican tomatoes with a nutritious starch.

INGREDIENTS (MAKES 8 ENTOMATADAS)

- 4 Roma tomatoes, 1 lb.
- 1 clove garlic
- 1/4 small onion, 1 1/2 oz.
- 1/2 tsp. fresh Mexican oregano or 1/8–1/4 tsp. dried oregano
- 1/4 bay leaf
- 1/2 cup water from boiling the tomatoes
- 1 tsp. salt
- 8 corn tortillas
- thin onion slices for garnish
- Cashew crumble (p. 158) (optional)

METHOD

1. Boil the tomatoes and onion for 15 minutes.
2. In a blender, place the tomatoes, onion, garlic clove, oregano, salt, and 1/2 cup water from boiling the tomatoes, and blend to make a smooth purée.
3. In a saucepan, add the tomato purée and the bay leaf and bring to a boil. Reduce the heat and simmer for 20 minutes. Taste and adjust the salt.
4. To assemble the entomatadas, pour the tomato sauce into a large skillet and place a large plate next to the skillet. Using two spatulas, dip a tortilla in the warm tomato sauce for about 8 seconds to infuse it with the tomato sauce. Be mindful that if you leave it too long, the tortilla may fall apart. Lift from the skillet and place it on the plate, folded in half. Serve 2 folded entomatadas per plate. Spoon more tomato sauce on each plate and serve immediately, topped with onion slices and, if desired, sprinkled with cashew crumble (p. 158).

TAMALES DE HONGOS | MUSHROOM TAMALES

The umami flavor of mushrooms in this dish is pumped up with the red chile and spices. Make these tamales for special celebrations, even Christmas, and they will be a hit. They can be served together with another vegan recipe, tamales de frijol, that I included in my cookbook, *Truly Texas Mexican: A Native Culinary Heritage in Recipes*.

Although lard is much used today in the making of tamales, neither pork nor lard is the most traditional way of celebrating family Navidad tamaladas. Spanish pigs did not initially receive a warm welcome from native peoples. Historians describe the pigs as carriers of the diseases that were responsible for the death of 90–96 percent of the native populations in the US, a devastating number. In the northern state of Coahuila, both the Pausan and Julime native communities did not eat pork. They did raise pigs but used them for trade with non-natives (Zadik, 2005).

In this traditional plant-based recipe, the combination of chiles, corn masa, and mushrooms gives Navidad a celebratory return to our delicious culinary roots.

INGREDIENTS (MAKES 12–16 TAMALES)

- 1 1/2 lbs. baby bella mushrooms, quartered
- 2 Tbs. canola or vegetable oil
- 1/2 tsp. salt
- water for steaming the tamales

FOR THE CHILE PASTE

- 3 chiles anchos
- 3 guajillo chiles
- 1 large clove garlic
- 3/4 tsp. cumin seeds
- 1 1/2 tsp. salt
- 1/2–3/4 cup water
- 1 Tbs. canola or vegetable oil
- additional water for soaking chiles

FOR THE MASA

- 2 1/4 cups masa harina (corn flour)
- 1 1/2 tsp. salt
- 1 3/4 cups water
- 1/2 cup canola oil, hot
- 1 Tbs. chile paste
- 12–16 dried corn husks that have been rehydrated

METHOD

Submerge the dried corn husks in a large bowl of water and soak them for 1–2 hours or overnight.

TO MAKE THE FILLING

1. In a large skillet, heat 2 Tbs. vegetable oil on high. When the oil begins to become wavy, add the mushroom quarters and sauté them until the edges are golden and crisp, about 10 minutes. Set aside and allow them to cool.

2. When the mushrooms are cool, place them in a food processor, along with 1/2 tsp. salt, and pulse to make a smooth paste that still has some bits of texture. Taste and adjust the salt as needed. Set aside.

TO MAKE THE CHILE PASTE

1. Deseed and devein all the chiles. Place them in a medium saucepan, cover with water, and bring to a boil. Turn off the heat, cover the saucepan, and hold for 20 minutes to rehydrate the chiles.
2. In a blender, place the rehydrated chiles along with the garlic, cumin, salt, and 1/2 to 3/4 cup water, enough for the blender to run smoothly. Blend until the paste is completely smooth. This may take up to 1 minute on high speed.
3. In a large saucepan, heat 1 Tbs. canola or vegetable oil, then add the chile paste, being careful with any splatter as the chile paste meets the hot oil. Fry the chile paste for 5–8 minutes until the color has deepened and the flavors combined. Most of the liquid will evaporate, leaving a thick paste that is not runny at all. Set aside.

FOR THE MASA

1. In an electric mixer, place the masa harina, salt, water, and 1 Tbs. of the chile paste. Mix until the ingredients combine to form a dough.
2. Turn off the mixer. Heat the oil on medium heat and when it is hot, add it very slowly and carefully to the dough in the mixer, being careful to prevent splattering.
3. Turn on the mixer to the lowest setting and blend the oil into the masa; increase the speed as the oil is incorporated. When the oil is fully incorporated, mix on high for 15–20 seconds. Transfer to a bowl and set aside.

TO ASSEMBLE THE TAMALES

1. Remove the corn husks from the water and shake to remove excess water. Trim each one so that the wide edge is about 6 inches.
2. Place 3 Tbs. of the masa onto each husk and spread it evenly starting about 3 inches from the pointed tip all the way to the wide end.
3. Spread 1 tsp. of the chile paste onto the masa, making a stripe lengthwise. Then, add 2 Tbs. of the mushrooms on top of the chile paste stripe, forming a lengthwise ridge in the middle of the husk. Fold the husk over the filling, rolling it like a cigar. Fold the pointed end down on the side that is opposite the seam. This will keep the tamal from unfolding.
4. Steam the tamales in a steamer for 45 minutes to 1 hour.

TIP: Place a penny in the water of the steamer so it makes a clinking noise. If it stops clinking, you need to add more water.

The tamales are cooked when the masa peels off the husk easily.

TAMALES DE HABAS Y RAJAS DE CHILES POBLANOS

Habas are lima beans, and like all beans, when combined with corn to make a tamal, they provide a complete protein, excellent nourishment for the body (Staff, 2011). Habas are native to Guatemala and travelled from there northward to Texas and elsewhere around the world (Stephens, 2018). This recipe is inspired by my college summer stay in Tehuantepec, Mexico, just south of Oaxaca before reaching the border with Guatemala.

Tamales de habas are served in that region, and I want to share this recipe in my Texas Mexican cookbook as just another way of emphasizing that from time immemorial Texas and Mesoamerica have been in communication. Down south they don't include rajas (strips) in the filling, and they don't flavor their masa at all. But here in Texas we do flavor the masa, and I think adding rajas makes the tamal pop.

INGREDIENTS (MAKES 12–16 TAMALES)

FOR THE FILLING

- 12 oz. frozen lima beans
- 1/2 cup white onion, diced
- 1 large clove garlic, minced
- 2 Tbs. canola or vegetable oil
- 1/4 bay leaf
- 2 cups water
- 1/2 tsp. salt
- 2 poblano chiles

FOR THE MASA

- 2 1/4 cups masa harina (corn flour)
- 1 1/2 tsp. salt
- 1 3/4 cup water
- 1/2 cup canola oil, hot
- 1/2 tsp. dried, powdered thyme (dried thyme can be crushed in a mortar to make a powder)
- 12–16 dried corn husks that have been rehydrated
- water for steaming

METHOD

Submerge the dried corn husks in a large bowl of water and soak them for 1–2 hours or overnight.

TO MAKE THE FILLING

1. In a large skillet, heat 2 Tbs. vegetable oil, then add the diced onion and sauté for 3–4 minutes. Add the garlic and cook for 30 seconds. Add the frozen lima beans, water, salt, and bay leaf and boil for 15–18 minutes until most of the liquid has evaporated. Remove the bay leaf.
2. Place the lima bean mixture in a food processor and pulse to make a completely smooth paste. Transfer to a bowl and set aside.

TO MAKE THE POBLANO CHILE RAJAS

1. Place the 2 poblano chiles under a broiler until the skin blisters, about 5 minutes, then turn over and do the same to the other side.
2. Cover the chiles with a damp cloth and let stand 15 minutes to soften the skin.
3. When the chiles have cooled, remove the stem and peel off the skin that has been softened and will be easy to peel. Remove all the seeds. Slice lengthwise into 1/4-inch-wide strips. Set aside.

FOR THE MASA

1. In an electric mixer, place the masa harina, salt, thyme, and water. Mix until the ingredients combine to form a dough.
2. Turn off the mixer. Heat the oil on medium heat and when it is hot, add it very slowly and carefully to the dough in the mixer, so as to prevent splattering.
3. Turn on the mixer to the lowest setting and blend the oil into the masa; increase the speed as the oil is incorporated. When the oil is fully incorporated, mix on high for 15–20 seconds. Transfer to a bowl and set aside.

TO ASSEMBLE THE TAMALES

1. Remove the corn husks from the water and shake to remove excess water. Trim each one so that the wide edge is about 6 inches.
2. Place 3 Tbs. of the masa onto each husk and spread it evenly starting about 3 inches from the pointed tip all the way to the wide end.
3. Place 2 to 3 Tbs. of the lima bean mixture, forming a line ridge in the middle of the husk, and then lay 2 poblano chile strips on top. Fold the husk over the filling, rolling it like a cigar. Fold the pointed end down on the side that is opposite the seam. This will keep the tamal from unfolding.
4. Add water to a steamer and steam the tamales for 45 minutes to 1 hour.

TIP: Check periodically to make sure that the water has not completely evaporated from the steamer. You can also place a penny in the water of the steamer so it makes a clinking noise. If it stops clinking, you need to add more water.

The tamales are cooked when the masa peels off the husk easily.

MESQUITAMAL

This sumptuous tamal dish made a splash at a historic gathering of Texas Mexican chefs who presented contemporary culinary showcases of comida casera, the home-style cooking of Texas Mexican American families. Called "Encuentro: The Native American Roots of Texas Mexican Food," it was held in Houston, Texas, in May 2023.

Chef Luna Vela of Austin, Texas, and Monterrey, Mexico, presented this dish in one of the culinary showcases. She stated that this dish emphasizes her ancient and continuing relationship to the mesquite tree and mesquite pods. Chef Vela explained that she was inspired to explore mesquite after reading the book *La gente del mezquite* by Dr. Manuel Valdés, which details the importance of mesquite as a food source and cultural symbol for our ancestors long before corn arrived in our region from Mesoamerica (Valdés, 1995).

Chef Vela's creation is to be served with pecan/mesquite mole (mole de nuez y mezquite, p. 48) and cactus pico (nopal pico de gallo, p. 156). Make each of these three recipes first and then serve them together as originally designed by Chef Luna Vela and described below.

INGREDIENTS (MAKES 12 TAMALES)

- 2 1/4 cups masa harina (corn flour)
- 1 3/4 cups water
- 3/4 cup mesquite flour
- 4 tsp. salt
- 1 tsp. baking powder
- 1 cup vegetable shortening
- brown vegetable stock, as needed (p. 171)
- 18 corn husks
- optional accompaniments: mole de nuez y mezquite (p. 48) and nopal pico de gallo (p. 156)

METHOD

1. Soak corn husks in warm water for 20 minutes or until soft and pliable.
2. Mix together the masa harina with 1 3/4 cups water to make a pliable masa (dough). Set aside.
3. In a stand mixer, whip vegetable shortening until fluffy, light, and creamy. Add salt and baking powder and slowly incorporate the masa and mesquite flour little by little at a gentle speed. When fully incorporated, mix for 5 minutes. Add brown vegetable stock (p. 171), 1 Tbs. at a time, until the dough reaches a soft, spreadable consistency.

TO ASSEMBLE THE MESQUITAMALES

Dry off the corn husks and on the smooth side, place 3 Tbs. of masa, forming a line that stretches lengthwise on the husks, leaving bare about 3 inches of the pointed tip of the husk. Wrap the husk to cover the masa. Fold the pointed tip opposite the seam to keep the seam closed. Stand each tamal, folded tip down and open end up, in a steamer basket with 1 inch of water, forming a circle of standing tamales leaning inward. Place some corn husks on top, then a kitchen towel, and cover with a tight-fitting lid. Steam on high heat for 45 to 50 minutes. Check the water periodically and add additional water as needed.

The tamales are now ready to serve with mole de nuez y mezquite (p. 48) and nopal pico de gallo (p. 156).

To serve the tamal, place it on a serving plate and partially open the corn husk to reveal the tamal. Pour mole de nuez y mezquite on top, then garnish with the nopal pico de gallo.

TOSTADAS

INGREDIENTS (MAKES 6 TOSTADAS)

- 6 corn tortillas
- 1 Tbs. vegetable oil (optional)

METHOD

Preheat oven to 350°F

TOSTADAS WITHOUT OIL

Place the tortillas on a cookie sheet and bake for 15–20 minutes until the color deepens to a dark tan and the tostadas are crispy. If the tostadas are not cooked long enough, they will be chewy rather than crispy.

TOSTADAS WITH OIL

Brush both sides of the tortillas lightly with vegetable oil. Place them on a cookie sheet and bake for 15–20 minutes until the color deepens to a dark tan. As above, if the tostadas are not cooked enough, they will be chewy rather than crispy.

Mesquitamal (photo by Amador Moe Lerma)

TOSTADAS DE BERENJENA

Most tostadas are layered with mashed pinto beans, so this is a twist away from that tradition, taking a turn that showcases the versatility of eggplant. It's actually not a vegetable but a fruit because it grows from a flowering plant and contains seeds.

Eggplants are a nutrient-dense food, containing vitamins and minerals with only 20 calories per cup. They are high in fiber and deliver antioxidants that reduce the risk of heart disease (Ajmera, 2017). They are delicious with the crunch of corn tostadas and the underlying herbaceous flavor of serrano chile.

INGREDIENTS (MAKES 4 TOSTADAS)

- 1 lb. eggplant, peeled, small dice
- 6 oz. white onion, small dice
- 5 oz. Roma tomatoes, small dice
- 2 cloves garlic
- 1 Tbs. extra virgin olive oil
- 1 serrano chile, 3 inches long, deseeded, deveined, minced very fine
- 1 tsp. fresh Mexican oregano, minced, (1/3 tsp. dried)
- 1 Tbs. fresh parsley, minced
- 3/4 cup white vegetable stock (p. 172)
- 1/2 tsp. salt
- 1/8 tsp. freshly ground black pepper
- 4 tostadas, store-bought (without trans fats) or made from the recipe on p. 32

GARNISH

- 1/2 cup red bell pepper, small dice
- 1 tsp. olive oil
- 1/8 tsp. salt
- pinch of dried thyme

METHOD

1. Prepare 4 tostadas (p. 32) or use store-bought tostadas. Set aside.
2. In a small skillet, heat 1 tsp. olive oil over medium to low heat, then add red bell pepper, salt, and a pinch of dried thyme. Cook for 8–10 minutes until the bell pepper is soft and has acquired black spots. Set aside.
3. In a medium saucepan, heat 1 Tbs. olive oil over medium heat. Add the onion and cook for 3–5 minutes until it is soft and transparent. Add the garlic and cook for an additional 1 minute. Add the eggplant and tomatoes and cook for 5 minutes, stirring occasionally.
4. Add the vegetable stock, serrano chile, oregano, parsley, salt, and black pepper and simmer for about 10 minutes, until the eggplant is fully cooked and soft but not mushy. The liquid will evaporate, leaving a moist guisado. If it becomes too dry add water, 1 Tbs. at a time. Check and adjust the salt.
5. When the eggplant is cooked, divide it evenly among 4 tostadas. For garnish, top each tostada with the red bell pepper mixture. Serve immediately.

TACOS DE HONGOS | MUSHROOM TACOS

We did not eat mushrooms in our San Antonio Westside home, but the umami flavor in these tacos certainly would have been a hit when we would gather around our yellow Formica and chrome trim kitchen table. I discovered mushrooms when I was in high school, and then I'd make them at home, sautéed. I've come to realize that it would be irreverent not to serve mushroom tacos with tomato and serrano chile.

INGREDIENTS (MAKES 12 TACOS)

- 1 lb. cremini or other mushrooms, sliced
- 1/4 cup white onion, small dice
- 1 1/2 Tbs. garlic, minced
- 2 cups ripe tomatoes, small dice
- 2 serrano chiles, stems off, cut into thin strips
- 2 Tbs. canola or other vegetable oil
- 1 Tbs. fresh epazote or parsley or cilantro, chopped
- 12 corn tortillas
- 1/2 tsp. salt

METHOD

1. In a skillet, heat 2 Tbs. vegetable oil over medium heat, then add the onions and cook for 3 minutes until they begin to turn translucent. Add the garlic and cook for 1 minute. Add the tomatoes, mushrooms, chiles, and salt. Cook, uncovered, for about 10–15 minutes, until the tomatoes and mushrooms soften and the juices evaporate. Add the epazote or cilantro or parsley and mix thoroughly. Taste and adjust the salt. Set aside.
2. Using a comal (griddle) at 350°F, heat the tortillas by first dipping each tortilla in a bowl of water and then placing them on the hot griddle. Cook for about 1 or 2 minutes, then flip the tortilla and heat the other side. There should be dark brown or black spots on the soft tortillas. (Note: This step rehydrates and also roasts the tortillas, adding the aroma and flavor of roasted corn.)
3. Place the tortillas on a plate and fill half with the mushroom mixture and fold into a taco.

Serve immediately with either crema de cajú (p. 164) or chiles toreados (p. 124) or both.

TORTITAS DE PAPA WITH SALSA AND SALAD

This recipe is by Chef Luis Olvera, chef/owner of acclaimed Trompo restaurant in Dallas that, sadly, closed in 2024. He is also from Monterrey, where his mom would make tortitas de papa during the Catholic Lenten season, and he says: "Of all the foods in my mother's repertoire, tortitas de papa were my favorite!"

Chef Olvera omits the eggs in this recipe and serves it with a caramelized onion salsa and a bright salad. He explains that plant-based dishes don't need to mimic meat or fish or anything non-plant; they just need to be their flavorful best. He said that when he started to cook and eat plant-based foods, he "earned a great appreciation for 'eating clean,'" meaning not only eliminating animal products but also avoiding the use of processed foods.

These tortitas de papa are not just healthful, they are also visually attractive and make a perfect lunch or dinner when served with Chef Olvera's salsa and salad.

INGREDIENTS (SERVES 4)

- 2 large russet potatoes (unpeeled)
- 2 Tbs. cornstarch
- 2 chopped scallions (or 1/4 diced onion)
- 1 chile de árbol, finely crushed or powdered (optional if you don't want heat)
- 1 cup avocado oil
- Salt and pepper to taste

FOR THE SALSA

- 3/4 white onion, sliced
- 1 jalapeño, coarsely chopped
- 1 large tomato, coarsely chopped
- 2 cloves garlic, coarsely chopped
- 1/4 cup cilantro, coarsely chopped
- 1/2 cup water
- Salt to taste
- 2 Tbs avocado oil

FOR THE SALAD

- 1 lettuce, shredded
- 1 tomato, sliced or wedged
- 1/2 cucumber, coarsely chopped
- 4 radishes, diced
- juice of 1 lime
- salt to taste

METHOD

1. In a large saucepan, place washed potatoes and add enough water to reach 2 inches above the potatoes. Bring to a boil, then lower the heat and simmer for about 30 minutes. Pierce with a fork to make sure they are cooked and tender. Cook another 5 minutes if the center is still hard. Drain the potatoes and when they are cool enough to handle, peel off the skin by rubbing firmly. The skin should slide off easily, but you can use a butter knife to scrape off the skin if that becomes necessary.

2. In a large mixing bowl, add the skinned potatoes, scallions or onions, cornstarch, chile de árbol, salt, and pepper, and mix with a strong spoon or your hands. The mashed mixture will be somewhat stiff.
3. Form the mash into golf ball–sized balls and flatten them to 1/2-inch thickness.
4. In a skillet, heat the oil over medium-high heat, gently add the patties, and fry them until they are golden on each side. Drain them on paper towels.

TO MAKE THE SALSA

1. In a skillet, heat the oil over medium heat, then sauté the onion slowly until it is caramelized, turning a deep golden brown.
2. In a blender, add the jalapeño, garlic, tomato, cilantro, and water and blend for a few seconds so that the ingredients combine but still retaining bits of texture rather than blending into a smooth purée.
3. Add the blended mixture to the caramelized onions and cook until heated through. Add salt and pepper to taste. Set aside, keep warm.

TO MAKE THE SALAD

Place the salad ingredients and lime juice in a bowl, add salt to taste, and toss to combine well.

To serve, distribute the tortitas de papa among 4 plates and top with the hot salsa. Add the salad on the side and enjoy a delicious traditional Lenten treat.

CHILE CON JACKFRUIT

Jackfruit takes beautifully to this combination of three chile flavors with aromatic spices. It is thought to have originated in India and is a nutritional superstar: high in protein, potassium, and vitamin B. I'm finding it more prevalent in grocery stores and online, already peeled, deseeded, and ready to cut up for this recipe. But if you are able to source the fruits intact, it's fun to work with. Make sure it is a young fruit, before the natural sugars have had time to develop.

Fun fact: it is the largest tree fruit in the world, capable of reaching 100 pounds. The fruit grows both on the branches and on the trunk of trees that can reach up to 50 feet. I'm including it here because I want to incorporate this delicious, although strange-looking, fruit into the flavor profile of our cuisine.

INGREDIENTS (SERVES 6)

- 11 oz. package young jackfruit
- 4 ancho chiles
- 3 guajillo chiles
- 2 chipotle chiles
- 2 cloves garlic, unpeeled
- 1 small white onion, peeled
- 1/2 tsp. cumin seeds
- 1 tsp. fresh Mexican oregano, packed tightly
- 1 Tbs. piloncillo, scraped, packed tightly
- 1 Tbs. canola oil
- 2 tsp. salt

METHOD

1. Drain and rinse the jackfruit. Pull apart the jackfruit into 1 inch–1 1/2-inch pieces or cubes. In a large skillet, heat 1 Tbs. canola oil and sauté the jackfruit until the pieces start turning a golden brown, about 8–10 minutes. Set aside and keep warm.
2. To devein the chiles, first lay the chile flat on a cutting board and, using a paring knife, cut a slit lengthwise. Then grab the chile with one hand and with the other break off the stem. Open the chile along the slit and remove the seeds and veins.
3. In a large saucepan, cover the cleaned chiles with water and bring to a boil. Turn off the heat and let the chiles steep for 15 minutes so that they rehydrate and become tender. Drain the chiles, discarding the water. Set aside to cool.
4. Heat a comal (griddle) or cast iron skillet on high, and then roast (i.e., no oil) the onion and the unpeeled garlic until the onion has softened and has black spots. Peel the garlic after it has cooked and become soft.
5. Place the onion, garlic, chiles, cumin, oregano, and salt in a blender, and blend to a very fine paste. To blend well, you will need to add 1/2–1 cup water.
6. In a Dutch oven, heat 1 Tbs. canola oil and add the chile paste. There will be splatter, so be prepared for it, keeping a lid nearby to cover the pan halfway as needed. Cook for 10 minutes, stirring all the while.

7. Add the browned jackfruit, 3 cups water, and piloncillo and bring to a very slow simmer. Cover and cook for 2 hours, all the while adjusting the heat so that it stays at a slow simmer. Stir occasionally to prevent the bottom from sticking. Uncover and cook for about 30 more minutes to thicken. The sauce should be thick enough to coat the jackfruit. Adjust the salt.

Serve with plant-based pan de maíz (cornbread).

PIPIÁN RANCHERO WITH JERUSALEM ARTICHOKES (SUNCHOKES)

Jerusalem artichokes are the tubers of a specific sunflower, *Helianthus tuberosus*, that was an everyday food of our Coahuiltecan ancestors in the land now occupied by San Antonio, Texas. The Tap Pilam Coahuiltecan Nation regularly holds ceremonies and cooking feasts on their ancestral homeland, where there has been continuous human habitation of the Tap Pilam Coahuiltecan people for over 15,000 years (Thoms & Mandel, 2007).

I want our community to reclaim this tuber that has more protein than corn, wheat, soybeans, and other beans. Amazingly, it also has a high level of inulin, which is a prebiotic fiber with medicinal properties. It can stimulate growth of bifidobacteria, which fights harmful bacteria and helps reduce certain carcinogenetic enzymes. It also contains many vitamins and is a very good source of minerals and electrolytes (Sandborn, 2016). Our ancestors cooked this superfood in earth ovens, right there in San Antonio, which is also known by its native name, Yanaguana.

Also called sunchokes, Jerusalem artichokes are a beautiful topping for this pipián ranchero which is a recipe from the Mexican state of Durango.

INGREDIENTS (SERVES 4)

FOR THE PIPIÁN

- 5 oz. chiles anchos
- 2 chiles de árbol
- 4 Tbs. (1 oz.) masa harina (corn flour)
- 2 cloves garlic
- 1 tsp. cumin seeds
- 3 cups water
- 2 tsp. salt
- 1 Tbs. canola oil

FOR THE JERUSALEM ARTICHOKE (SUNCHOKES)

- 1/2 lb. Jerusalem artichoke
- 1 Tbs. canola oil
- 1 cup water
- salt to taste
- 12 5-inch corn tortillas

METHOD

1. Remove the stems from the chiles, but do not remove the seeds.
2. In a saucepan, add the dried chiles, with seeds, cover with water, and bring to a boil. Turn off the heat and let rehydrate for 15 minutes.

3. In a blender, place the rehydrated chiles with seeds, masa harina, garlic, cumin, and salt with 3 cups water. Process on high for 1 to 2 minutes to make a smooth, velvety purée. If there are still seeds or large particles, strain through a fine mesh sieve.
4. In a large saucepan, heat 1 Tbs. canola oil, then add the chile purée and cook for 12 minutes so that the flavors blend, the red color deepens, and the mixture thickens. Stir as needed to prevent the bottom from sticking. It should coat the back of a spoon. Set aside and keep warm.

FOR THE JERUSALEM ARTICHOKES

1. Wash the Jerusalem artichokes very well, making sure to remove all the dirt in the crevices of the little tubers. Brush lightly to remove some of the dark skin, then cut them into 1/4-inch slices.
2. Place the sliced Jerusalem artichokes in a 10-inch or 12-inch skillet. Add 1 cup water and 1 Tbs. canola oil. Bring to a boil, then turn down the heat and simmer, uncovered, for 15 minutes. Pierce to test if the tubers are fully tender. If they are not, add another cup of water and continue to cook, checking for doneness every 5 minutes. The sunchokes should be fork-tender but not mushy. Allow as much water to evaporate as possible but be careful not to burn the tubers. When they are fully cooked and tender, taste and add salt as needed. Set aside and keep warm.
3. Dip each tortilla in the heated chile purée for about 8 seconds so that it is saturated but not breaking apart. Using two spatulas, carefully transfer them, 3 per serving plate. Make sure there's a generous coating of pipián on each tortilla. Spoon additional hot pipián as needed.
4. Top each tortilla with the hot sunchoke slices. Serve immediately.

PIPIÁN VERDE WITH YUCCA AND CALABACITAS

Squash seeds, dried and mashed, are an ancient tradition in Mexican cooking, part of the native pre-Conquest diet all the way from Texas southward to Mexico City. The scientific name for the squash is *Cucurbita pepo*, and ancient remains dating back over 4,000 years have been found south of Brownsville, Texas, in the Mexican state of Tamaulipas. Older squash remains have been found also in Oaxaca, dating back 10,000 years (Vela, 2017).

Pipián revolves around seeds, mainly squash seeds, with chiles, tomatoes, and greens. It's a complex and beautiful celebration of plant-based traditions.

INGREDIENTS (MAKES 3 CUPS, SERVES 6)

- 9 oz. yucca
- 1 lb. calabacita or zucchini
- 1 Tbs. canola oil
- 4 1/2 cups water
- 1/4 cup roasted pumpkin seeds for garnish
- salt to taste

FOR THE PIPÍAN

- 1 oz. brown sesame seeds (white as a substitute)
- 1 1/2 oz. raw Spanish peanuts without the skin
- 1/4 lb. pumpkin seeds, hulled
- 1/4 cup additional pumpkin seeds
- 1/2 lb. tomatillos, peeled and washed
- 1/4 white onion, quartered
- 2 chiles serranos
- 2 cloves garlic, unpeeled
- 7 green lettuce leaves, torn into pieces
- 6 radish leaves, torn into pieces
- 1 large hoja santa, torn into pieces
- 1 Tbs. canola oil
- 1 tsp. salt
- 1 1/2 cups white vegetable stock (p. 172)

METHOD

TO MAKE THE PIPIÁN

1. In a skillet (no oil), toast the sesame seeds until they turn a golden brown. Set aside.
2. In the same skillet, toast the peanuts until they turn a dark golden color. Set aside.
3. In the same skillet, toast the pumpkin seeds until they begin to deepen in color, about 5 minutes. Overcooking the pumpkin seeds will make them bitter, so err on the side of less time than 5 minutes. Remove from the heat and set aside.
4. Roast another batch (1/4 cup) of roasted pumpkin seeds and set aside for garnish.
5. In a saucepan, cover the tomatillos with water, bring to a boil, and simmer for 10 minutes or until they turn a deep, earthy green.
6. In a cast iron skillet or griddle, place the

onion, garlic, and serrano chiles and roast them (no oil) until they become soft and develop black spots. Set aside, removing the skin from the garlic.

7. In a blender, purée the dry-roasted onion, garlic, serrano chiles, salt, and tomatillos, along with all the leafy greens. Add 1/2 cup or more water to make a smooth purée.
8. In a Dutch oven, heat 1 Tbs. canola oil and add the puréed tomatillo ingredients and cook for about 10 minutes until the green color deepens and the sauce thickens.
9. In a blender, add the sesame, peanuts, 1/4 lb. pumpkin seeds, and 1 1/2 cups water, and blend on high until a smooth purée forms.
10. Add the purée seeds and peanuts to the tomatillo mixture, adding 1 1/2 cups white vegetable stock, and simmer gently for 30 minutes so the flavors meld and the sauce thickens. It should not be runny and should coat the back of a spoon. Taste and adjust the salt.

TO COOK THE YUCCA AND CALABACITAS

1. Peel the yucca by first cutting off the ends. Using a sharp knife, make an incision lengthwise, just deep enough to reveal the dark skin and the thin white layer beneath it. Using your fingers, peel off the skin. You can also use a small knife to help cut off the peel. Slice the yucca into 1-inch rounds, then cut each round in half. Use a small knife to remove the tough root that is at the core of each slice.
2. In a saucepan, bring 4 1/2 cups of water to a boil. Add the yucca slices and boil for 10 to 15 minutes, until the yucca is completely cooked and tender when pierced with a fork. Drain well, transfer to a platter, season with salt, and hold warm.
3. Wash the calabacitas or zucchini and cut off the ends. Slice them lengthwise into quarters, then slice crosswise into 1/2-inch-thick wedges.
4. In a 12-inch skillet, heat 1 Tbs. canola oil on high heat. When the oil is hot but not smoking, add the calabacita wedges and sauté, tossing until they acquire a dark roasted color along the edges, about 3 to 5 minutes. The calabacita should be tender but still a bit firm. Do not overcook. Transfer to a platter, season with salt, and hold warm.

To serve, pour a generous amount of hot pipián onto each serving plate and then arrange the warm yucca and calabacitas on top. Garnish with the roasted pumpkin seeds.

ACORN SQUASH WITH MOLE

Sweetness from the acorn squash blends well with this mole that features chiles anchos, the dried version of the ripe chile poblano. Mole is ubiquitous in Texas and Northeastern Mexico, with many variations. It is mainly served with turkey or chicken, but it's really at home with this satisfying acorn squash.

In my younger days, it was common to buy prepared mole in a jar (every small neighborhood grocery store sold it) and then finish it at home by adding peanut butter or other ingredients. It was delicious and a fast route to making the dish that is served at weddings and other special occasions. I served mole at my 25th wedding anniversary and plan to do so at my upcoming 52nd wedding anniversary.

This mole recipe reminds me of the special place that Two-Spirit people like me have held in our communities, akin to the LGBTQ+ awareness of today. In many Native American communities across Texas and North America, Two-Spirit individuals—those who embody both masculine and feminine spirits—have historically held esteemed positions, particularly in the culinary arts. These individuals often transcended traditional gender roles: men embraced responsibilities typically associated with women, such as cooking and food preparation, while women took on roles traditionally held by men, such as hunting and warfare (Apache, 2017).

During community celebrations, Two-Spirit individuals were honored guests, their contributions to both the spiritual and physical nourishment of the community deeply respected. The recognition of Two-Spirit people reflects a broader Indigenous understanding of gender and sexuality as a spectrum, rather than a binary. Such inclusivity was integral to the social fabric of many tribes. Two-Spirit people were known as the keepers of tradition, storytellers, and healers, highlighting their multifaceted contributions to Indigenous societies (Carroll, 2022).

INGREDIENTS (SERVES 6)

- 1 acorn squash
- 6 chiles anchos
- 2 Tbs. canola oil or vegetable oil
- 1 small white onion, diced
- 5 cloves garlic
- 3 black peppercorns
- 2 whole clove buds
- 1 stick canela (Mexican cinnamon), 1 inch long
- 2 slices bread (no eggs or milk), torn into large pieces
- 2 Tbs. apple cider vinegar
- 1 tsp. salt
- 1 cup water
- 1 1/2 cups brown vegetable stock (p. 171)
- 2 Tbs. sesame seeds

METHOD

Preheat oven to 375°F

1. On a comal (griddle) over medium heat, roast the chiles until they start to change color and develop some black spots. Place the chiles in a saucepan and cover with water. Bring to a boil and then turn off the heat and let the chiles soak for 20 minutes. Set aside and drain before using.

2. Cut the acorn squash in half, lengthwise, using a heavy knife. Scoop out the seeds. Leave the peel intact. Place in a baking sheet, cut side down, and bake for 30–40 minutes. Check doneness by piercing with a fork. The squash should be cooked and tender but not mushy. When cool enough to handle, slice the squash into 1-inch slices, peel on.
3. In a skillet, heat 1 Tbs. oil over medium heat, then add the onion and cook for 5 minutes until it becomes translucent. Add the garlic and cook for 1 minute. Set aside.
4. Heat a dry skillet over medium heat. Add the sesame seeds and toast them for 2–3 minutes, swirling or stirring. As soon as their color starts to deepen and become golden, remove immediately and transfer to a cool plate. Set aside.
5. In a blender, add the chiles, black peppercorns, cloves, canela, and bread, along with the cooked onion and garlic. Add 1 cup water and blend on high until the purée becomes smooth and velvety. Strain through a fine mesh sieve to remove any particles.
6. In a Dutch oven or large saucepan, heat 1 Tbs. canola or vegetable oil, then add the chile purée. Keep a lid handy to block any splatter. Cook for 5 minutes until it thickens and the color deepens.
7. To the chile mixture, add 1 1/2 cups brown vegetable stock, 2 Tbs. apple cider vinegar, and 1 tsp. salt. Simmer for 10 minutes, then add the acorn squash slices and gently stir the squash to coat with the mole without breaking the slices. Cook for an additional 5 minutes until the squash is heated through.

Serve the acorn squash with plenty of mole and garnish with the sesame seeds. Serve with corn tortillas.

MOLE DE NUEZ Y MEZQUITE | PECAN AND MESQUITE MOLE

Chef Luna Vela's pecan and mesquite mole is a fresh take on the rich tradition of Mexican mole. In this recipe, she revitalizes indigenous flavors by incorporating two essential ingredients native to Texas and Northeastern Mexico: pecans and mesquite pods. The result is a deeply flavorful dish that honors the region's culinary heritage while offering a deliciously modern interpretation.

This is her advice about cooking mole: "Mole, regardless of where it's from or what regional tradition it comes from, is all about the time and care you put into layering each flavor and section of this sauce. This is about the attention you give it, and how you choose to honor those ingredients, at the end bringing them together harmoniously and letting them sing their song of the land."

INGREDIENTS (MAKES 1 QUART)

- 1 Tbs. Mexican oregano
- 1 Tbs. black peppercorn
- 1 Tbs. allspice
- 1 Tbs. coriander
- 1 six-inch cinnamon stick
- 6 Tbs. sesame seeds
- 6 ancho chiles
- 12 guajillo chiles
- 1 tsp. chiltepin / chile piquín
- 10 tomatoes, roasted
- 1 1/2 white onion, roasted
- 2 garlic heads, unpeeled, roasted
- 3 Tbs. mesquite flour
- 2 Tbs. corn masa
- 1–2 Tbs. vegetable oil
- 1/4 cup grapeseed oil or other neutral oil
- 6 Tbs. pecans
- 1 quart brown vegetable stock (p. 171)
- salt to taste

METHOD

Preheat oven to 350°F

1. In a comal (griddle) or cast iron skillet, roast all the chiles for 3–5 minutes until they develop black spots. Set aside.
2. In the same comal (griddle) or skillet, roast the oregano, black peppercorn, allspice, coriander, and cinnamon stick for 3–5 minutes until they are aromatic. Grind the spices in a molcajete (mortar) or spice grinder. Set aside.
3. Preferably over mesquite charcoal or wood, or under a broiler, roast the tomatoes, garlic, and onion so that they develop a charred exterior but are not burned. Peel the garlic and place it in a blender along with the tomatoes, onions, and chile piquín. Blend until smooth. Set aside.
4. In a Dutch oven or large pan add 1–2 Tbs. vegetable oil, enough to cover the bottom, and turn the heat to high. Add the tomato mixture, placing a lid as needed to control the splatter. Stir often and let the mixture come to a boil, then reduce to a simmer. Cover and let cook for 1-2 hours until reduced by half.

5. In a separate Dutch oven or large pan, add the grapeseed or other neutral oil and the pecans. Bring the heat to medium and cook for 6-8 minutes or until the color begins to deepen.
6. Add the sesame seeds, stirring often so as to not burn. After 1 minute, add the roasted chiles, then the mezquite flour, the corn masa, and the ground spices. Stir well to combine.
7. Add the vegetable stock and deglaze the bottom of the pan. Allow the mixture to cool, then place in a blender and blend to create a silky purée. Add more vegetable stock to the blender as needed. If there are any large particles in the purée, strain through a fine mesh sieve.
8. Add the strained purée to the tomato mixture and cook over low heat for 1-2 hours until the consistency is thick, coating the back of a spoon. Taste and correct the salt.

This mole is meant to be paired with mesquitamal (p. 30). But you can also use it as a sauce for sautéed chayote (p. 123) or sautéed Jerusalem artichokes (p. 131).

CHAPTER 2

FILETES, TORTAS, GORDITAS, TOSTADAS

Cauliflower filet (photo by author)

CABBAGE AND POTATO GORDITAS

Gorditas, when paired with beans, make a complete protein that nourishes your body, but the combination is also a time-tested flavor binary. There are very few basic flavor binaries—that is, two ingredients that taste so good together they are truly a match made in heaven. The two-ingredient combination of refried pinto beans with gorditas or corn tortillas is one of those delicious flavors that you can eat just as is.

In this dish, the traditional binary gets a robust splash from cabbage in red sauce. It's a gordita I love to share.

INGREDIENTS (MAKES 12 GORDITAS)

- 4 cups masa harina (corn flour)
- 3 1/2 to 4 cups water
- 4 cups cooked pinto beans
- 2 lbs. cabbage, core removed and sliced thinly
- 12 oz. waxy potatoes, peeled, small dice
- 7 oz. red bell pepper, stem off, deseeded, small dice
- 5 oz. bulb green onions, sliced crosswise into 1/4-inch rounds
- 2 serrano chiles, stems off, sliced lengthwise in half, then sliced crosswise into half-moons
- 1 Tbs. extra virgin olive oil
- 1/2 tsp. salt
- olive oil to coat the griddle for the gorditas

FOR THE BROTH

- 12 oz. tomatoes, quartered
- 4 oz. tomatillos, quartered
- 2 cloves garlic
- 1 tsp. cumin seeds
- 1/2 tsp. black peppercorns
- 1 tsp. salt
- 1 cup water

METHOD

TO MAKE THE BEANS

In a skillet, over medium heat, place the cooked pinto beans with 1/2 cup water and mash them with a potato masher until they are smooth but retaining some texture. Cook them for 15–20 minutes, scraping the bottom of the skillet as the beans roast and develop flavor. No oil is needed. Add water, 1/4 cup at a time, if they become too dry. They should be a little runny but not soupy. Set aside and keep warm.

TO MAKE THE CALDITO (BROTH)

In a blender, place the tomatoes, tomatillos, garlic, cumin seeds, black peppercorns, salt, and 1 cup water and blend until completely smooth. Set aside.

TO MAKE THE POTATO DICE

1. In a small skillet, place the diced potatoes and add water to cover them. Add 1/2 tsp. salt and 1 Tbs. olive oil and mix to

combine. Cook on medium heat until the water boils, then lower the heat to a simmer and cook until the water evaporates.

2. When the water has evaporated, the potatoes should be slightly cooked but still firm.
3. Continue cooking, sautéing the potato over medium heat, so that the dice develop a golden color. Cook until they are soft and set aside, warm.

TO MAKE THE CABBAGE

1. In a large skillet or Dutch oven, heat 1 Tbs. olive oil. Add the red bell pepper and sauté for 5 minutes. Then add the green bulb onion and serrano chiles and sauté for 5–6 minutes. The onion will soften and become translucent.
2. Pour in the caldito, bring to a boil, then lower the heat and simmer, covered, for 10 minutes. Taste and adjust the salt.
3. Add the cabbage and mix thoroughly. If the mixture is too dry, add water, 1/2 cup at a time. Bring to a boil, then lower the heat, cover, and cook at a low simmer for 15–20 minutes, until the cabbage is completely cooked and soft. As with the beans, the cabbage should be a little runny but not soupy. Taste and adjust the salt.

TO MAKE THE GORDITAS

1. In a large bowl, mix the masa harina and add the water gradually to make a soft, pliant masa. You may not need all the water.
2. Divide the masa into 12 balls, then mold them with your hands into 4-inch patties that are 1/2-inch-thick gorditas.
3. Heat a comal (griddle) on medium heat, then coat with a light film of olive oil. Place the gorditas on the griddle and cook for 2 minutes, then flip them and cook the other side for 2 minutes. They will have a golden color. Flip them again so that each side cooks for an additional 3–4 minutes, on medium to low heat. Hold them warm.

To serve, slice each gordita in half and apply a generous layer of mashed pinto beans to each half. Lay the halves on a plate and dollop with a portion of the cabbage, then dot the top with the potato dice. Serve hot.

CAULIFLOWER FILETS WITH PARSLEY SALSA

Fresh vegetables were a constant at our family kitchen table, and when the cool of spring and fall came around, cauliflower was always present. Amá would wash and separate the florets, then boil or sauté them. Serrano chile salsa was invariably on the table, so in this recipe I recall those days of enjoying cauliflower accompanied by serrano salsa.

Even though both of my parents have passed away, as have six of my eight brothers and sisters, with this dish I can conjure them as family and warmly recall our time together. Cauliflower and serrano chile together hold those memories for me.

Making filets—some call them cauliflower steaks—is a brilliant way to a sumptuous meal and maybe will also make memories.

TIP: Save the florets and you can serve them another time as roasted cauliflower florets, using this same recipe.

INGREDIENTS (MAKES 4–6 FILETS)

- 2 cauliflower heads
- 1/2 cup extra virgin olive oil
- 2 tsp. paprika
- 1 tsp. thyme
- 1 tsp. salt

FOR THE PARSLEY SALSA (MAKES 2 CUPS)

- 3/4 cup extra virgin olive oil
- 1/2 cup red wine vinegar
- 1 1/2 Tbs. parsley, finely minced
- 1/2 Tbs. fresh Mexican oregano
- 1/4 Tbs. serrano chile, deseeded, deveined, minced
- 1 tsp. salt

METHOD

Preheat oven to 400°F

1. In a bowl, whisk together the olive oil, red wine vinegar, parsley, Mexican oregano, serrano chile, and salt until emulsified. Set aside.
2. In a bowl, whisk together 1/2 cup extra virgin olive oil with paprika, thyme, and salt. Set aside.
3. Wash the cauliflower heads and remove all the leaves. Place each head stem side up and slice into 1/2-inch–3/4-inch filets. There will be 2 or 3 filets per head, depending on their size.
4. Brush both sides of the filets generously with the paprika and thyme mixture. Use the brush to coat all the crevices.
5. Place the filets on a baking sheet and bake for 15 minutes, then turn them over and bake for another 10 minutes. Remove when they are cooked and have acquired a rich roasted color. They should be fork-tender and golden brown.

Serve the filets either on a platter or individual plates and then pour a long, wide strip (cordón) of the salsa over them.

HERBED CORN AND JERUSALEM ARTICHOKE TART

The Jerusalem artichoke is not an artichoke. It's a type of sunflower called *Helianthus tuberosus*, and it grows readily all over Texas and Northeastern Mexico. This sunflower does not have a long taproot but instead produces tubers that look like little potatoes, ginger root, or water chestnuts. The tubers do have a slight taste resemblance to the heart of an artichoke.

The plant has nothing to do with Jerusalem. In Spanish, sunflower is girasol, and maybe someone thought that sounded like Jerusalem. It's also called sunchoke.

I love the combination of corn with the taste of sunchokes, especially with a splurge of aromatic herbs. On a bed of thick poblano salsa, it makes a delicious course. Although this is more complicated than other recipes in this book, I recommend making it as a special gift for someone you love.

INGREDIENTS (MAKES 6 TARTS)

- 12 oz. (2 cups) frozen corn kernels
- 2 Tbs. extra virgin olive oil
- additional olive oil for greasing cake pan and molds
- 1/4 tsp. salt
- 6 oz. (1 cup) Jerusalem artichokes, sliced into 1/4-inch dice/pieces (peeling them as a visual preference is optional)
- 1 cup water
- 1 Tbs. canola oil
- 1/8 tsp. dried thyme
- 1/8 tsp. dried basil
- 1/8 tsp. dried Mexican oregano
- 1/8 tsp. chile sal (p. 161)

FOR THE THICK CHILE POBLANO SALSA

- 1 poblano chile
- 1/4 cup water
- 2 tsp. crema de cajú (p. 164)
- 1/4 tsp. salt

METHOD

Preheat oven to 350°F

1. In a blender, place the corn kernels, olive oil, and salt and blend until the corn kernels are broken down to a paste. There will still be some textured particles. If needed to blend properly, add 1 or 2 Tbs. water.
2. Grease a small cake pan with olive oil and add the corn paste, distributing it evenly. Bake in a 350°F oven for 25–30 minutes until the corn is cooked and the color deepens. Allow the corn cake to cool.
3. In a mixing bowl, using a large fork, combine the corn cake with the thyme, basil, oregano and chile sal. You may need to use your fingers to combine well. Set aside.
4. Wash the Jerusalem artichokes very well, brushing them to remove all the dirt in the crevices of the little tubers. Use a potato peeler to remove all the skin, then cut them into 1/4-inch dice.

5. Place the diced Jerusalem artichokes in a saucepan, adding 1 cup water and 1 Tbs. canola oil. Bring to a boil, then turn down the heat and simmer, uncovered, for 15 minutes. Pierce to test if the tubers are fully tender. If they are not, add another cup of water and continue to cook, checking for doneness every 5 minutes. Allow as much water to evaporate as possible, but be careful not to burn the tubers. When they are fully cooked and tender, taste and add salt as needed. Set aside and keep warm.

TO MAKE THE THICK CHILE POBLANO SALSA

1. Place the chile poblano under a broiler and cook for about 5 minutes, until the skin blisters, turning slightly brown with some black spots. Flip and do the same to the other side. Remove from the broiler and cover completely with a damp cloth for 15 minutes.
2. When cool enough to handle, peel the outer paper-thin skin from the chile. Make a slit in the chile, lengthwise, to open it and remove all the seeds and the stem.
3. Place the peeled chile in a small blender or food processor with 1/4 cup water and blend until completely smooth. Add 2 tsp. crema de cajú and combine until smooth. Adjust the salt and set aside in a small saucepan.
4. Use 2 1/2-inch diameter tart rings to assemble the tarts. Oil the inside of the rings with olive oil. Press 2 Tbs. of the herbed corn cake in the ring, then top with 2 Tbs. of the Jerusalem artichoke, pressing lightly. Place the tarts in an oiled baking dish and cover with aluminum foil. They can be baked immediately or stored in a refrigerator for several hours.
5. When ready to serve, place the aluminum-covered tarts in a 350°F oven for 20 minutes until heated through. Divide the thick chile poblano salsa among 6 plates, then unfold the tarts on top. Sprinkle the tarts with chile sal.

HIBISCUS FLOWER DROWNED TORTA

This delicious torta is drowned by dipping it into a tomato salsa. You can still eat it messily with your fingers or you can opt for utensils. The second salsa, with chile piquín, adds a boost of flavor.

Both salsas are flavored with Texas Mexican oregano, *Poliomintha longiflora*, which is native to Texas and the northern Mexican states of Nuevo León, Coahuila, and San Luis Potosí. Thriving in hot climates, it produces striking clusters of small pink or lavender bell-shaped flowers. As a member of the mint family, it brings a wonderful flavor to my dishes. Unfortunately, it is not available in grocery stores. It grows abundantly in my garden, and I encourage you to consider planting it, whether in a garden bed or a pot.

Poliomintha longiflora is a different flavor, brighter and lighter than the more commercially available Mexican oregano, *Lippia graveolens*, which belongs to the verbena family and grows farther south into Central and Southern Mexico. Because it is widely available in stores, it is readily used in Texas Mexican cooking as well. Fragrant and flavorful, it remains a valuable ingredient in the kitchen.

Oregano plays a crucial role in the flavor profile of Texas Mexican cuisine, making it important to distinguish between the two herbs commonly known as Mexican oregano. Today only the Mexican oregano is sold in grocery stores because over time many families have forgotten to use our own plant, a result of our growing habit to source our herbs from corporate grocery stores. In the Westside of San Antonio, where I grew up, *Poliomintha longiflora* was grown in our neighborhood front and backyards. My extended family used this oregano and not the *Lippia graveolens*.

I suggest you plant some in your garden. The plants are sold in nurseries with the names of rosemary mint or Mexican oregano. It is a perennial bush with lovely, happy pink flowers. When making this dish, I love to go outside, pick a few sprigs, and enjoy being with nature.

INGREDIENTS (SERVES 4)

- 4 tortas or 1 baguette, cut crosswise into 5-inch pieces
- 1 cup cooked pinto beans

FOR THE TOMATO SALSA

- 8 oz. Roma tomatoes, quartered
- 1 1/2 oz. white onion, coarsely chopped
- 1 clove garlic, whole
- 1/4 tsp. dried Mexican or Texas Mexican oregano
- 1 Tbs. canola oil

FOR CHILE PIQUÍN SALSA

- 7 chiles piquín
- 2 Roma tomatoes, coarsely chopped
- 1 1/2 oz. white onion (1/4 small onion), coarsely chopped
- 1 clove garlic, whole
- 1/4 cup white vinegar

- 1/2 tsp. dried Mexican or Texas Mexican oregano
- 1 cup water
- salt to taste

FOR HIBISCUS

- 1/2 cup hibiscus flowers, rinsed
- 3/4 oz. white onion, diced
- 1 clove garlic, minced
- 1/4 tsp. dried thyme
- 1/4 laurel leaf, the size of a thumb
- 2 cups water

METHOD

TO MAKE THE TOMATO SALSA

1. In a blender, place the tomatoes, onion, garlic, and oregano and blend until smooth.
2. In a saucepan, heat 1 Tbs. canola oil, then add the tomato mixture and cook for about 8 minutes, until the color deepens. Set aside and keep warm.

TO MAKE THE CHILE PIQUÍN SALSA

1. In a saucepan, add 1 cup of water and all the other ingredients. Bring to a boil and simmer slowly for 20 minutes. Allow to cool slightly.
2. In a blender add the cooled ingredients (including all the liquid) and blend until smooth. Adjust the salt and set aside to cool.

TO COOK THE BEANS

In a skillet, over medium heat, place the cooked pinto beans with 1/2 cup water and mash them with a potato masher until they are completely smooth but retaining some texture. Cook them for 15 minutes, scraping the bottom of the skillet. Add a little water if they become too dry. Set aside and keep warm.

TO COOK THE HIBISCUS FLOWERS

In a saucepan, add 2 cups of water and the hibiscus flowers, onion, garlic, thyme, and laurel leaf and bring to a boil. Simmer for 25 minutes. Remove the laurel leaf and set aside.

TO ASSEMBLE THE DROWNED TORTAS

1. Slice each torta or baguette piece horizontally in half leaving one crusty end still connected, so that it folds.
2. Spread the bottom half with 2 Tbs. beans and 1 Tbs. hibiscus flowers, then fold both sides together. Using tongs, dip the torta in the tomato sauce to coat the outer surface. Transfer to a serving plate.

Serve the drowned tortas accompanied with the chile piquín salsa.

MILANESA DE ZUCCHINI CON SALSA DE RÁBANO | ZUCCHINI CUTLETS WITH RADISH SALSA

Zucchini cutlets become crispy on the outside and mouthwateringly tender inside. They make an eye-pleasing dish, and the tomatillo radish salsa adds color and flavor brightness.

INGREDIENTS (SERVES 4)

- 2 zucchini (12 oz.)
- 3/4 cup flour
- 1/2 tsp. baking powder
- 1/8 tsp. salt
- 1/2 cup water
- 2–3 cups peanut oil
- 1/2 cup flour for dredging

FOR THE SALSA

- 9 oz. tomatillos, peeled, washed, and quartered
- 1 clove garlic
- 1/4 oz. white onion
- 2 tsp. chile serrano, minced
- 1/4 tsp. salt
- 1 cup radish, thinly sliced and cut into 1/4-inch squares/pieces

METHOD

1. In a blender, add the tomatillos, garlic, onion, chile serrano, and salt and blend until fairly smooth but not creamy. Transfer to a bowl and add 1 cup of thin radish squares. Taste and correct the salt. Set aside.
2. In a shallow bowl, combine 3/4 cup flour, baking powder, salt, and water and whisk together to make a smooth batter. Set aside.
3. Wash the zucchini and cut off the ends. Slice lengthwise to make 1/4-inch-thick slices. Set aside.
4. In a deep skillet, add peanut oil to a depth of 1/4 inch. Heat the oil until it reaches 350°F. If you don't have a thermometer, spoon a pea-size drop of batter. If it sizzles and rises to the top, the temperature is right. If it turns brown immediately, the oil is too hot, so take it off the heat for a minute before proceeding.
5. When the oil is the right temperature, dredge a slice of zucchini in 1/2 cup flour to coat, then shake off all the excess. Using

tongs, dip the zucchini into the batter to coat well, then place in the oil and let it cook for 2–3 minutes, until the batter begins to brown slightly. Turn over and cook the other side. The total time will be about 6 minutes, and the batter will be a deep golden color. Transfer the zucchini to a platter lined with paper towels.

6. Cook all the zucchini this way, making sure not to crowd the skillet and that the oil does not cool down nor become too hot.

Serve on individual plates or on a platter and pour a wide strip (cordón) of the radish salsa over the zucchini cutlets. Serve at room temperature.

MEMELAS OAXAQUEÑAS

These memelas from Oaxaca are a thinner, flatter version of our Texas Mexican sopes, the small, shallow corn masa casseroles filled with well-fried beans. While Oaxaca and Texas may seem distant from one another today, the connection between these regions dates back thousands of years. Archaeological finds—including black obsidian from the Mesoamerican region of Oaxaca discovered in Texas—reveal that exchange routes linked these regions for at least 3,000 years. Along with goods, these networks facilitated the exchange of culinary traditions, reinforcing the long-standing cosmopolitan nature of Texas Mexican food (Hester, n.d.).

Including memelas in this collection recognizes how our Texas Mexican cuisine is deeply intertwined with Mesoamerican foodways. Like sopes, memelas rely on the flavorful pairing of pan-roasted beans and freshly made salsa to make the masa shine. The memelas and beans can be prepared a day in advance since they reheat well and retain their flavor, but the salsa and lettuce should be prepared fresh, keeping in the fridge for up to 6 hours if necessary.

INGREDIENTS (MAKES 15 MEMELAS)

- 2 cups masa harina (corn flour, not corn meal)
- 2 cups water
- 1 cup cooked pinto beans
- 1/2 cup water, plus 2–3 Tbs. additional water as needed
- 1 cup very thinly sliced iceberg lettuce threads
- 1/2 cup queso de almendras (p. 159) (optional)

FOR THE SALSA

- 2 tomatoes, diced
- 1 serrano chile, minced
- 1/4 cup white onion, minced
- 1/2 tsp. salt

METHOD

1. In a skillet, over medium heat, place the cooked pinto beans with 1/2 cup water and mash them with a potato masher until they are completely smooth but retaining some texture. Cook them for 15 minutes, scraping the bottom of the skillet. Add an additional 2 or 3 Tbs. water if they become too dry. Set aside and keep warm.
2. In a bowl, combine the diced tomato, onion, minced chile, and salt. Set aside.
3. Combine the masa harina with the water and mix thoroughly. Cover with a damp cloth and let rest for 15 minutes so that the corn rehydrates. Make little balls, about 15, with the masa.
4. Heat a comal (griddle) to medium high, 375°F.
5. Flatten the balls, one by one, using a tortilla press lined with a clean plastic sheet similar to a grocery bag. To flatten the corn tortilla, cover the bottom of the tortilla press with one half of the plastic and place one of the balls in the middle. Fold the other half of the plastic over the ball. Press once, gently. Then turn the

plastic-wrapped tortilla 180° and press gently a second time. The tortilla should be about 1/4-inch thick, no thicker.

STEPS FROM THE TORTILLA PRESS TO THE COMAL (GRIDDLE)

1. Gently peel off the plastic from the top of the corn tortilla.
2. Remove the tortilla from the press and place the uncovered side in one hand.
3. With your other hand, peel off the plastic from the other side.
4. Release the tortilla from your palm as you roll it onto the comal (griddle).
5. Cook the tortilla for about 1 minute, until it begins to turn a golden brown. Then use a spatula or your fingers to flip it and cook the other side for a minute. Remove the tortilla from the comal and, while it is still warm, crimp it all around with your fingers, forming a crimped wall, about 1/2-inch high, all around the edges of the tortilla. Set aside the memelas until ready to assemble and serve.
6. To assemble the memelas, first reheat them by laying them on the hot comal until they are heated through. Then fill them with a layer of the beans, followed by a generous layer of the thin iceberg lettuce threads, and top with the tomato salsa. Sprinkle with queso de almendras, if using.

Serve immediately.

CHAPTER 3

SOUPS AND SALADS

AJOBLANCO | CHILLED GARLIC SOUP

Ajoblanco is an ice-cold soup from the southern Andalusía region of Spain. I include this recipe as my nod to Spain's influence, even though this soup is hardly known at all in our Texas Mexican region. It predates gazpacho, that other, better known Spanish cold soup that is based on tomatoes imported from Mexico after the conquest.

The English translation of ajoblanco is white garlic, and it's indeed a beautifully white soup made with only 4 ingredients: almonds, garlic, olive oil, and hearty bread. It is humble, and so delicious.

There is general agreement that the soup is part of the Andalusía regional cuisine, and two towns in that region, Málaga and Granada, have an ongoing dispute, both claiming to have invented ajoblanco. The town of Almáchar, just east of Málaga, holds the annual Fiesta del ajoblanco on the first Saturday of September.

I first tasted this Spanish garlic soup in Madrid as the first course of a summer lunch. It has a rich, creamy consistency that comes from the blanched almonds that are traditionally mashed in a mortar, but that can be easily puréed in a blender, as in this recipe. Traditional garnish is the white (green) Muscat grape, plentiful in Málaga, as are almonds.

INGREDIENTS (MAKES 6 CUPS)

- 4 oz., by weight, raw almonds
- 5 1/2 oz., by weight, day-old bread that has a dense crumb and crusty exterior
- 1 quart ice-cold water
- 1/2 cup Spanish (or other) extra virgin olive oil
- 2 cloves garlic
- 2 Tbs. white wine vinegar
- 1/2 tsp. salt or to taste
- 18 seedless white (green) grapes, halved

METHOD

1. Wash the seedless grapes and cut them in half, lengthwise. Set aside for garnish.
2. To peel the skin off the almonds, place the almonds in a pot of boiling water for 60 seconds, no more. Drain them in a colander and rinse them with cold water to cool. Blot the almonds dry, then press them between your fingers to peel off the skin. Set aside. (Note: You can skip this step if you purchase almonds that have already been blanched and peeled.)
3. In a blender, add the almonds, garlic, and 2 cups water. Blend until the almonds are liquefied, with no granules.
4. Add the bread, white wine vinegar, extra virgin olive oil, salt, and remaining water and blend until completely smooth.
5. Chill the soup in the refrigerator for two hours or overnight.

Taste and adjust the salt. If you want a thinner consistency, add a little more cold water, according to your preference.

To serve, pour the cold soup into bowls and garnish with the grape halves.

COLD MANGO SOUP

This delicious soup is both savory and sweet, and it provides a remedy when the days bring on relentless heat. The sweetness of mango is tempered by the acid of vinegar and a bit of onion, and I think you'll like the refreshing taste of cucumber.

INGREDIENTS (MAKES 4 CUPS)

- 2 medium mangos (14 oz. of pulp)
- 4 oz. cucumber, peeled, quartered
- 3/4 oz. white onion
- 2 oz. extra virgin olive oil
- 2 tsp. white vinegar
- 1/2 tsp. salt
- 2 cups water

FOR GARNISH

- 4 Tbs. cucumber, sliced into 1/4-inch dice
- 1 Tbs. chile sal (p. 161)

METHOD

1. Peel the mangos and cut off all the pulp away from the pit.
2. In a blender, place the mango pulp, peeled cucumber, and all the other ingredients (excluding the garnish ingredients) and blend for about 1 minute until smooth and creamy.
3. Chill the soup for 4 hours or until it is completely chilled.
4. When ready to serve, gently toss 4 Tbs. of cucumber dice in 1 Tbs. chile sal so that the dice are completely coated.

To serve, pour the chilled soup in 4 bowls and float 1/2 Tbs. of the chile sal cucumber dice on each bowl as garnish.

Garbanzo and calabacita soup with chipotle (photo by author)

GARBANZO AND CALABACITA SOUP WITH CHIPOTLE

Garbanzos and the Mexican tatuma squash make an excellent combination in this soup, getting a flavor pop from the chipotle chile. A salad combination of these two ingredients is on p. 96 using a vinaigrette. These dishes are reminders of the cosmopolitan nature of our cuisine: garbanzos native to the Mediterranean and tatuma squash native to Northeastern Mexico and South Texas.

INGREDIENTS (SERVES 8)

- 1 15 oz. can garbanzo beans, drained
- 3 oz. white onion, small dice
- 1 medium carrot, small dice
- 1 celery stalk, small dice
- 1 Tbs. extra virgin olive oil
- 1 medium, 8 oz. tatuma or zucchini squash, medium dice
- 1 bay leaf
- 1/3 cup chopped cilantro leaves
- 1/2 tsp. salt
- lime slices for garnish

FOR THE CALDITO (LIQUID)

- 12 oz. Roma tomatoes
- 4 oz. white onion, quartered
- 2 cloves garlic
- 1 cup water

METHOD

1. In a large skillet, heat 1 Tbs. extra virgin olive oil over medium heat, then add the small dice of onion, carrot, and celery. Sauté for 5 minutes, until the onion is soft and translucent.
2. While the vegetables are cooking, prepare the caldito by placing the Roma tomatoes, white onion, and garlic in a blender with 1 cup of water. Blend on high to make a smooth purée.
3. Add the tomato purée to the vegetables in the skillet, along with 1 bay leaf and 1/2 tsp. salt, and bring the mixture to a boil. Lower the heat to a simmer and cook for 8–10 minutes for the flavors to develop.
4. Add the garbanzo beans and simmer for another 10 minutes.
5. Add the diced squash and cook for 5–7 minutes until it is fork tender. Taste and adjust the salt.
6. Turn off the heat and add the cilantro, stirring well.

Serve hot with fresh lime slices.

GREEN CORN SOUP

This soup is delicate but amazingly rich in flavor. To preserve the lovely green color that comes from tomatillos, poblano chiles, and other greens, I use white vegetable stock (p. 172), which also adds a bit of sweetness. It's a great way to celebrate the summer.

INGREDIENTS (SERVES 6)

- 1/2 cup white onion, cut into small squares
- 2 cloves garlic, minced
- 4 Tbs. extra virgin olive oil
- 2/3 cup tomatillos
- 1 1/2 lbs. corn kernels
- 4 cups white vegetable stock (p. 172)
- 2/3 cup green peas
- 6 cilantro sprigs with no stems
- 2 poblano chiles
- 3 romaine lettuce leaves, quartered
- 1 1/2 tsp. salt
- corn tortillas

METHOD

1. In a blender, place the tomatillos and blend until smooth. Set aside.
2. Place the poblano chiles under a broiler and cook until the skin blisters, about 5–10 minutes. Turn them over so all sides are charred. They will have some black spots, but make sure they don't burn. Remove them from the oven and cover with a damp cloth for 15 minutes. When they are cool enough to handle, peel off the paper-thin skin, then cut a slit along one side and remove the stem and all the seeds and white membranes. Set aside.
3. In a large saucepan, heat 4 Tbs. olive oil and add the onion. Cook for 2 minutes until it starts to become translucent, then add the minced garlic and cook for 30 seconds. Add the blended tomatillos and cook on medium heat for 5 minutes, stirring.
4. In a blender, place the corn, poblano chiles, green peas, cilantro, lettuce leaves, salt, and 2 cups of the vegetable broth. Blend on high until smooth and creamy. Add more broth as needed to blend properly.
5. Add the blended corn mixture and the remaining vegetable broth to the saucepan and bring to a boil. Lower the heat and simmer the soup for 20 minutes. Keep scraping the bottom to make sure it is not burning.

Serve the soup with corn tortillas. The soup can be cooled and refrigerated for 5 days.

POSOLE ROJO

Posole, spelled pozole in Southern Mexico regions, is a delicacy and one of my favorite dishes to serve at dinner parties. Cooked with special combinations of red chiles, it is a traditional dish that is cooked also by Native communities northwest of us, Pueblos in New Mexico, and Navajos in Arizona (Keegan, 2010). Most recipes make posole with pork, but this is more traditional, because pork arrived in Mexico and Texas only about 500 years ago, so for centuries before that, we were pork-less and loving it.

Making posole involves a process called nixtamalization, boiling large white, dry corn, called *maíz pozolero*, with calcium hydroxide (slaked lime) that results in hominy. Invented by Indigenous Mesoamerican women about 3,500 years ago along the present Guatemala and Mexico border, nixtamalization changes the chemical structure of the kernel, making niacin available in digestion and boosting the availability of protein (Towell, 2008).

When boiled in this red chile broth, the nixtamalized kernels pop open, creating a floret. If you don't have the time for nixtamalization, you can use canned hominy.

INGREDIENTS (SERVES 10)

FOR THE CORN

- 1 1/2 lbs. cacahuazintle (dried white corn for posole). This large white dried corn is available online or from an increasing number of Texas corn mills that perform nixtamalization to make tortillas and masa for tamales.
- 1 Tbs. calcium hydroxide (slaked lime)

FOR THE CHILE PASTE

- 3 guajillo chiles, deseeded and deveined
- 2 chiles ancho
- 3 cloves garlic
- 1 Tbs. dry Mexican oregano
- 1 tsp. cumin seeds
- 1 tsp. salt

ACCOMPANIMENTS

- 1/2 cabbage, sliced into thin strips (alternately, shredded iceberg lettuce)
- 1 bunch radishes, thinly sliced
- 1 cup white onion, small dice
- 3 Mexican limes, cut into wedges
- 1 bunch fresh cilantro, coarsely chopped

METHOD

FOR THE CORN

1. The night before, place the dry corn in a large pot and fill with water 4 inches above the corn. Soak overnight.
2. The following day, discard the water, then add clean water and the calcium hydroxide. Bring the water to a boil and boil the corn for 15 minutes. Check doneness by taking out one kernel and rubbing between your thumb and forefinger. If the outer, slippery skin rubs off easily, the corn is done. Let the corn soak in the water for 10 minutes, then drain.
3. Place the corn in a bowl or pot of clean water and vigorously rub the kernels together to scrape away the slippery skin from all the kernels. Change the water as

needed until you get no debris and the corn is clean and white. Some of the little brown seed germs on the kernel tips will fall off. That's very good, because they have to be removed.

4. Use your fingernails or a knife or scissors to take off the little brown seed germ (pedicel) at the tip of each kernel. This is labor intensive, but it will allow the kernels to bloom into little flowerets when they are boiled. I often leave the pedicel on because it adds fiber to the dish. Set aside.

FOR THE CHILE PASTE

1. Remove the seeds from the chiles by cutting a slit lengthwise in each chile to open it and remove the stem with the attached seeds. Remove all the other seeds in the chile pod.
2. Place the chiles in a large pot and cover them with water. Bring to a boil, turn off the heat, and let the chiles steep for 15 minutes so they will rehydrate. Drain and allow to cool. Discard the water.
3. Place the chiles, garlic, oregano, cumin, and salt in a blender. Add 1 cup of clean water and blend on high until the paste is completely smooth, with no large particles. It is okay to add a little more water if needed. If there are large particles in the paste after you are done blending, strain the paste through a fine mesh sieve.

TO BOIL THE POSOLE

Add the chile paste to the cleaned corn, adding enough water to cover 3 inches above the corn, and boil it for 1 hour or longer, up to 3 hours, depending on the quality of the corn, until the kernels burst open like little flower buds. If you have kids, they'll love this transformation.

Serve the posole in bowls accompanied by finely shredded cabbage, thinly sliced radishes, lime wedges, cilantro, and diced white onion. Accompany with warm corn tortillas.

POSOLE VERDE WITH MUSHROOMS

At dinner parties this is a dish that wows with its bright green color and herbal flavors. The history of pozole, spelled with an "s" in South Texas and Northeastern Mexico, begins 3,500 years ago in what is now Guatemala and Southern Mexico. Women transformed simple corn kernels into a nutrition-rich food through a molecular process that involves boiling dried corn with calcium hydroxide (slaked lime). The process is called nixtamalization. It turns corn kernels into hominy.

INGREDIENTS (SERVES 4)

- 3/4 lb. cremini mushrooms, washed, sliced
- 1/2 cup white onion, diced
- 3 cloves garlic, minced
- 2 poblano chiles
- 1 serrano chile
- 2 tomatillos, peeled, washed, and quartered
- 1/4 cup cilantro, chopped
- 1/2 cup chard, washed and chopped
- 1/8 tsp. dried Mexican oregano
- 1 1/2 quarts white vegetable stock (p. 172)
- 1 lb. hominy
- 1 Tbs. vegetable oil
- 1/2 cup roasted and ground pumpkin seeds (optional)
- 2 leaves of epazote (optional)

GARNISH

- 1 avocado, diced
- 4 radishes, washed, sliced
- 1 cup thinly sliced iceberg lettuce
- 4 tostadas (p. 32)

METHOD

1. In a Dutch oven, heat 1 Tbs. vegetable oil over medium-high heat. Add the sliced mushrooms and sauté for about 5 minutes, until they are soft, the edges a bit browned. Transfer the mushrooms to a bowl.
2. In the same Dutch oven, add the diced onion, lower the heat, and cook for about 4 minutes until the onion becomes translucent. Add the garlic and cook an additional 1 minute. Then return the mushrooms to the Dutch oven. Set aside.
3. Place the chiles poblanos under a broiler and cook them for about 5 minutes, until the skin blisters, turning slightly brown with some black spots. Flip them and do the same to the other side. Remove them from the broiler and cover completely with a damp cloth for 15 minutes.
4. When cool enough to handle, peel the outer paper-thin skin from the chiles. Slice each chile lengthwise to remove all the seeds and the stem. Set aside.
5. If you are adding the optional pumpkin seeds, use a cast iron or other skillet, on

medium heat, and roast the pumpkin seeds for about 5 minutes or until they start turning a golden color. Remove from the heat immediately. Overcooking them will develop a bitter taste. Set aside.

6. In the same skillet, on medium heat, roast the chile serrano and the tomatillos until they are soft and develop black spots, about 5–7 minutes. Set aside.
7. In a blender, add the poblano and serrano chiles, tomatillos, cilantro, chard, epazote (if using), and oregano and blend on high until the purée is smooth and velvety. Add 1/2 cup water as needed to blend the ingredients well.
8. In a saucepan, over medium heat, add the green purée and cook for 5 minutes until the color deepens to an earthy green. Then add the powdered roasted pumpkin seeds and combine well.
9. Add the cooked purée to the mushroom mixture in the Dutch oven; add the hominy and heat thoroughly.

Serve hot, accompanied with tostadas and garnishes so that each diner may enjoy according to their preference.

SOPA DE CALABACITAS

Whether you use heirloom tatuma squash or the zucchini that came later, this calabacita soup has vigorous flavor not just from the sautéed golden squash but also from the roasted vegetables. Little golden balls made from corn masa take this soup over the top as a sumptuous brunch meal unto itself.

INGREDIENTS (SERVES 8)

- 3 Roma tomatoes
- 1 white onion, 1/2-inch-thick slices
- 1 clove garlic, unpeeled
- 2 Mexican tatuma squash or zucchini, washed and diced
- 4 cups brown vegetable stock (p. 171)
- salt to taste
- 1 1/2 cups masa harina (corn flour, not corn meal)
- 1 cup water
- 1/4 tsp. salt
- 1/2 cup canola or vegetable oil
- 1 Tbs. canola or vegetable oil
- 3 leaves epazote (optional)

METHOD

1. On a comal or griddle, medium heat, roast the tomato, onion slices, and garlic for about 5 minutes, turning them as needed until the vegetables are cooked. They will develop dark spots. Peel the garlic.
2. In a blender, add the tomato, onion, and garlic and blend until smooth. Set aside.
3. Mix together the corn flour, 1/4 tsp. salt, and water to make a masa. Then shape the masa into little balls that are 1 inch in diameter. There will be about 25.
4. In a skillet, heat the oil over medium heat until it begins to shimmer with waves. Add the masa balls and fry them until they become golden brown and the masa is cooked, turning them as needed, about 5 minutes. Set aside to drain on paper towels.
5. In a skillet, heat 1 Tbs. oil over high heat, then add the diced zucchini and cook until it develops a slightly golden color. Turn down the heat to medium and add the tomato, onion, and garlic mixture. Cook for 5 minutes, then add the vegetable stock, salt, and epazote. Bring the soup to a boil, then remove the epazote if you used it and turn off the heat. Taste and adjust the salt.
6. Drop the fried masa balls into the soup, stirring to combine.

Serve immediately.

SOPA DE ELOTE

For fall and winter days this is always a go-to, winning soup. Roasted green poblano chiles are especially distinctive when immersed in the delicious yellow corn broth with veggie stock.

INGREDIENTS (SERVES 6)

- 1 1/2 lbs. (4 cups) fresh or frozen corn kernels
- 2 cups water
- 1/4 cup extra virgin olive oil
- 3 cups white vegetable stock (p. 172)
- 1 1/2 tsp. salt
- 2 poblano chiles
- 6 corn tortillas
- 2 Tbs. extra virgin olive oil for brushing on the tortillas

METHOD

Preheat oven to 350°F

1. Place the poblano chiles under a broiler and cook until the skin blisters, about 5–10 minutes. Turn them over so all sides are charred. They will have black spots, but make sure they don't burn. Remove them from the oven and cover with a damp cloth for 15 minutes. When they are cool enough to handle, cut a slit along one side and remove the stem and all the seeds and white membranes. Slice them lengthwise into 1/2-inch strips, then slice them crosswise into 1/2-inch squares. Set aside.
2. Brush both sides of each corn tortilla with olive oil, then slice the tortillas into 1/2-inch strips. Slice the strips crosswise to make 1/2-inch squares. Place the squares on a baking sheet in a single layer and bake in a 350°F oven for 5–10 minutes until the squares turn a deep golden brown. Watch closely so that they do not burn. Set aside.
3. In a blender, place the corn kernels and 2 cups of water and blend until completely smooth with no granular particles.
4. In a large saucepan, heat the olive oil over medium heat, then add the corn mixture and cook for 5 minutes, stirring as needed so that the bottom does not burn.
5. Add the vegetable stock and salt and bring to a boil. Then lower the heat and simmer for about 15 minutes.

To serve, place 1 Tbs. of the roasted poblano squares in the bottom of bowls. Pour the soup over them, then top with sprinkles of the tortilla squares.

SOPA TARASCA

Los Tarascos, the Tarascan people, are a civilization dating back over 2,000 years in the region of what is now the state of Michoacán and parts of Guanajuato, Guerrero, and Jalisco (Schöndube, 2017). Although this soup does not belong to the traditions of Northeastern Mexico, I've decided to include it for two reasons. First, I've developed many friends in Michoacán and that is exactly what our ancestors did when over centuries they travelled back and forth, exchanging knowledge and recipes with each other, making friends. Second, I love this combination of pinto beans with tomato purée and want to share it.

INGREDIENTS (SERVES 4)

- 1 cup dried pinto beans (boiled for 4 hours)
- 1/4 small white onion
- 1 clove garlic
- 2 Tbs. canola or vegetable oil
- 2 Roma tomatoes, quartered
- 1/2 white onion, chopped
- 1 clove garlic, minced
- 1 1/2 cups brown vegetable stock (p. 171)
- 1/2 tsp. salt
- 2 guajillo chiles, deseeded, sliced into thin strips
  6 corn tortillas
- 1/4 cup canola or vegetable oil

METHOD

Preheat oven to 350°F

1. In a large saucepan, add the dried beans, 1/4 small onion, and garlic clove, and enough water to cover 2 inches above the beans. Bring to a boil and cook for 4 hours or until the beans are completely soft. You can reduce the cooking time by as much as half by soaking the beans overnight prior to cooking them. While cooking, keep adding small amounts of water as needed so that the beans do not become dry. Set aside.
2. On a cookie sheet, lay the 6 corn tortillas in a single layer and brush both sides with oil. Bake for 15–20 minutes until the tortillas turn a dark tan color. Set aside.
3. Remove the stem from the chiles and remove all the seeds. Slice into thin strips. Set aside.
4. In a skillet, heat 2 Tbs. oil over medium heat. Add the chopped onion and cook for 4 minutes until it becomes translucent; add the minced garlic and the tomatoes and cook until the tomatoes are fully cooked and soft.
5. In a blender, add the tomato mixture and the beans and blend until completely smooth. Transfer to a large pot and add 1 1/2 cups brown vegetable stock. Cook over low heat, simmering slowly for 15 minutes.

To serve, ladle the soup into bowls. Break apart the baked tortillas into migas (crumbs) and distribute the pieces among the bowls, along with 5 or more of the chile strips.

Sopa tarasca (photo by author)

Avocado and kidney bean salad (photo by author)

AVOCADO AND KIDNEY BEAN SALAD | ENSALADA DE AGUACATE CON FRIJOL

The adjective "creamy" does not require actual cream from cows, as this recipe clearly demonstrates. The bite of white kidney beans is naturally smooth and creamy. Together, kidney beans and avocado make a wonderfully bright and, yes, creamy salad.

INGREDIENTS (SERVES 4)

- 1 large Haas avocado, small dice
- 1 medium red bell pepper, small dice
- juice of 1/2 lime
- 1 Tbs. cilantro, chopped
- 1 cup white kidney beans
- 1 small serrano chile, minced
- 1/4 tsp. salt

METHOD

1. Place the avocado, red bell pepper, serrano chile, and cilantro in a bowl and mix gently so that the avocado dice do not get smashed.
2. Add the beans, lime juice, and salt and combine well. Taste and adjust the salt.

Serve immediately at room temperature or chill for 1 hour.

CACTUS AND BEAN SALAD | ENSALADA DE NOPALITOS CON FRIJOLES

You'll never go wrong pairing these two ancient and iconic ingredients, cactus and beans. They are as natural as you can get. The Caddo people, known as the Hasinai kingdom, grew beans and traded them with other Texas Indigenous groups. A Spanish priest who lived among the Caddo people, Fray Francisco Casañas de Jesús María, reports in 1691 that the Caddo farmers planted at least five varieties of beans ("Tejas > Caddo Fundamentals > Caddo Life," n.d.).

Cactus, of course, has been integral to our culture for more than 9,000 years. Evidence of cactus is found in Hinds Cave, a unique and important archaeological site, near Del Rio, Texas. Our Texas ancestors not only ate the nutritious cactus paddles and the prickly pear fruit but also used the dried pads as pouches for carrying stuff. Hinds Cave has flooring mats that are made of dried cactus paddles dated to 6400 BC. The floor mats were used to cover the dusty floor ("Nature-prickly pear," n.d.). The spines, of course, were removed.

INGREDIENTS (SERVES 6)

- 1/4 lb. (1/2 cup) dried pinto beans
- 1 clove garlic
- 1/2 tsp. salt
- 2 cups water
- 1 lb. nopalitos, small dice
- 1 cup water
- 1 tsp. salt
- 1 cup tomato, small dice
- 1/2 cup red onion, small dice
- 1 Tbs. green chile serrano, minced

FOR THE VINAIGRETTE

- 1/4 cup extra virgin olive oil
- 2 Tbs. fresh lime juice
- 1 tsp. raw agave nectar
- 1 tsp. fresh Mexican oregano, minced
- 1/4 tsp. salt or to taste

METHOD

1. In a saucepan, add 2 cups of water, beans, garlic, salt, and bring to a boil. Turn the heat to low, cover, and boil for about 90 minutes to 2 hours, or until the beans are soft. Watch the beans regularly and add water as needed. Allow the beans to cool, then drain. Save the water to make bean soup or for enfrijoladas (p. 23).
2. In a saucepan, add the diced nopalitos, 1 cup of water, and 1 tsp. salt and bring to a boil. Turn the heat to low and simmer for about 15 minutes or until most of the water has evaporated. Set aside and allow the nopalitos to cool.

TO MAKE THE VINAIGRETTE

Whisk together the olive oil, lime juice, agave nectar, salt, and minced oregano until it emulsifies. Alternately, place in a jar and shake vigorously.

TO MAKE THE SALAD

Mix together the drained beans, drained nopalitos, tomatoes, onion, and chile serrano. Add the vinaigrette and mix thoroughly. Adjust the salt as desired.

Serve at room temperature or chilled.

NOPALITOS ASADOS CON VINAGRETA AL GUAJILLO

Nopalitos are often pickled (en escabeche), but here the vinegar is only a dressing. The roasted cactus are drizzled with a vinegar dressing that is flavored with guajillo chiles, echoing the traditional hot dish, nopalitos with red chile (p. 134). This makes a wonderful appetizer, letting your guests slice off portions and enjoy with corn tortillas.

INGREDIENTS (SERVES 8)

- 4 nopalitos (cactus paddles), cleaned of spines. Some stores sell the nopalitos already cleaned, so it is convenient to purchase those. Just make sure that they are fresh, firm, and bright green.

FOR THE VINAGRETA

- 1/2 cup extra virgin olive oil
- 1/4 cup apple cider vinegar
- 3 chiles guajillos, deseeded, deveined
- 1 tsp. salt

METHOD

1. To clean the nopalitos, place newspaper sheets, parchment, or other paper on a cutting board to catch the spines, some of which are powdery and can attach to the skin. Using tongs and a sharp knife, cut out all the spines from the cactus paddles. The spines are on little bumps, which helps in cutting them out. Rinse the nopalitos and carefully discard the spines.
2. Make incisions (do not slice) in the middle of each cactus paddle, lengthwise, 1/2 inch apart, starting1/2 inch from the top and ending 1/2 inch from the bottom. Fold the cactus paddles lengthwise in half, loosely, so that the incisions create folded ribbons. Arrange the folded paddles side by side on a round platter, the thin portion in the center, forming a large floweret.
3. Place all the vinagreta ingredients in a blender and blend on high until smooth and emulsified.
4. Pour the vinagreta in the center of the floral pattern, then use a brush or spoon to cover the entire surface of the nopalitos.

Serve at room temperature or chilled.

Nopalitos asados con vinagreta al guajillo (photo by author)

Botana de xoconostles (photo by author)

BOTANA DE XOCONOSTLES

Xoconostle is not to be confused with the tuna, although both are fruits of nopales (cactus). They have the same shape, but the tuna turns a bright magenta when it ripens, while the xoconostle turns a pale pink. Tunas are sweet and xoconostles are very tart, which is a perfect taste in this savory appetizer, botana, to enjoy with your favorite beer.

Your palate will love the taste of this botana, and your body will get a refreshing, healthy dose of nutrition, including high fiber, minerals, vitamin C, and antioxidants (Secretaria de Agricultura y Desarrollo Rural, n.d.). While it is in fact highly nutritious, with your margarita or beer you'll just enjoy it as a delicious botana.

INGREDIENTS (SERVES 6)

- 1 jícama, 12 oz. (2 1/2 cups), diced
- 14 oz. (2 cups) xoconostle, diced
- 2 Tbs. white onion
- 3 Tb red or green jalapeño chiles, minced
- 1/2 tsp. dried Mexican oregano
- 1/4 tsp. dried thyme
- 2 Tbs. lime juice
- 1/2 tsp. salt

METHOD

1. Peel and cut the jícama into 1/4-inch cubes. Set aside.
2. Slice the xoconostles in half and spoon out the seeds at the center. Using a spoon, scoop out the flesh and cut into 1/4-inch cubes. Set aside.
3. In a bowl, mix the jícama, xoconostle, white onion, jalapeño chiles, oregano, thyme, lime juice, and salt. Cover and refrigerate for 30 minutes or longer for the flavors to meld and develop.

Serve chilled or at room temperature as a botana to accompany beer or margaritas.

ENSALADA DE CALABACITA

Tatuma is the heirloom squash that's been living on this planet for over 10,000 years. Called calabacita, it's a variety of the *Cucurbita pepo* species, originating in and native to Northeastern Mexico (Castellanos-Morales et al., 2019). Zucchini is a better-known type of *Cucurbita pepo* variety, developed around the mid-1800s in Italy. It has a different flavor, with some bitterness. I don't prefer it for this ensalada, but it still makes a fine dish, so it's a good option if you can't find the Mexican tatuma, calabacita.

Tatuma is full-flavored, with some sweetness and no bitterness. It has been generously nourishing us as it moved to all parts of the world as the result of the violent European conquest of Northeastern Mexico and Texas. Today, tatuma can bring us together, at a table where all will be welcome.

INGREDIENTS (SERVES 4)

- 1 lb. Mexican tatuma squash or zucchini
- 1/2 white onion, thinly sliced
- 1 Tbs. extra virgin olive oil
- 1/2 cup lime juice
- 1 avocado, sliced
- 4 Tbs. (1/4 cup) pitted green olives

FOR THE VINAGRETA

- 3 Tbs. extra virgin olive oil
- 3 Tbs. lime juice
- 1/8 tsp. dried Mexican oregano
- 1 tsp. dried thyme
- 1/8 tsp. freshly ground black pepper
- 1/4 tsp. salt

METHOD

1. Wash the squash and slice it lengthwise into quarters, then slice into 2-inch strips.
2. Sauté the squash in the oil for about 5 minutes, until they are cooked tender but still firm. Set aside to cool.
3. In a bowl, add 1/2 cup lime juice and the onions, and let the onions marinate for 30 minutes until they are wilted. Set aside.
4. In a bowl, whisk together the vinagreta ingredients until emulsified. Add the squash and combine thoroughly.

Serve the squash on a platter and garnish with the avocado slices, wilted onions, and olives.

Ensalada de calabacita (photo by author)

ENSALADA DE CALABACITA Y EJOTE

As in other recipes, squash and beans just go together so well. I like the crispness that green beans add to this salad, and the pomegranate seeds are a fun surprise. There's no mistaking that the combination of extra virgin olive oil and lime juice provide a flavor base that is typically Mexican.

INGREDIENTS (SERVES 6)

- 12 oz. tatuma squash or zucchini
- 6 oz. green beans
- 3 oz. white onion, thinly sliced
- 1 avocado, sliced
- 1 Tbs. extra virgin olive oil
- 1/4 cup pomegranate seeds (optional)

FOR THE VINAGRETA

- 3 Tbs. extra virgin olive oil
- 3 Tbs. fresh lime juice
- 1/8 tsp. dried thyme
- 1/8 tsp. dried Mexican or Texas Mexican oregano
- Pinch of ground black pepper

METHOD

1. Wash the tatuma or zucchini and slice off the ends. Slice lengthwise into quarters, then slice into 2-inch strips. In a skillet, sauté the slices in 1 Tbs. olive oil for about 5–7 minutes until they are cooked but still firm. Set aside.
2. Wash the green beans and cut them into thirds. In a saucepan of boiling water, cook them for about 8 minutes until they are fully cooked but still firm. Drain and set aside to cool.
3. In a bowl, whisk together the vinagreta ingredients until emulsified, then add the pomegranate seeds (if using).
4. Gently toss squash, green beans, and onions with the vinagreta until fully combined.

Serve with slices of avocado.

This salad can be served at room temperature or chilled for several hours.

ENSALADA DE GARBANZOS Y CALABACITAS

Garbanzos team up with calabacita to make a delicious salad. Squash was first cultivated in Texas and Northeastern Mexico, so it's at home in this dish that features a guajillo chile vinaigrette. But garbanzo beans are also at home even though they come from the Mediterranean, including France and Turkey (Harvard T. H. Chan School of Public Health, 2018).

Both dried and canned garbanzos have a low glycemic index and low glycemic load, and they are an excellent source of carbohydrates, protein, fiber, B vitamins, and even minerals like iron and magnesium. So, this salad that marries a native ingredient with one from afar is full of health boosters and great flavor.

INGREDIENTS (SERVES 6)

- 4 medium-sized Mexican calabacitas or zucchini, sliced in quarter rounds
- 1 cup cooked garbanzos. Use canned or cook dried garbanzos. (Note: 1/2 lb. dried garbanzos makes 3 cups cooked.)
- 1 chile guajillo, deseeded, deveined, roasted
- 1 1/2 Tbs. balsamic vinegar
- 1 tsp. sugar
- 1 tsp. salt

METHOD

1. If you are not using canned garbanzos but cooking dried garbanzos, first pick over the garbanzos to remove any small rocks or debris, rinse, and drain. Place in a pot and add enough water to cover them by 2 inches. Bring them to a boil and cook for about 2–4 hours, depending on how dry they are. You can also soak them overnight so that the cooking time will be cut in half. They are cooked when the inside is soft but still a bit firm, not mushy. Allow the garbanzos to cool.
2. Remove the stem and seeds from the chile guajillo and dry roast on a griddle or cast iron skillet, medium heat, until it develops some black spots, about 2 minutes.
3. Place the chile in a pot, cover with water, and bring to a boil. Lower the heat and simmer for 15 minutes. Drain and discard the water.
4. In a blender, place the rehydrated chile, balsamic vinegar, sugar, and salt and blend to a smooth purée. Set aside.
5. Wash the calabacitas or zucchini and slice them into quarter slices, 1/4-inch thick.
6. Mix the calabacitas and the garbanzos together with the chile purée dressing.

Serve immediately.

Ensalada de garbanzos y calabacitas (photo by author)

LEEKS IN TOMATILLO SALSA

Leeks are a type of onion (*allium*), originally grown in the Eastern Mediterranean region over 4,000 years ago. They look beautiful, and the flavor is mild, pairing well with this tomatillo sauce.

Leeks are a cousin to the wild onions that are native to Texas and Northeastern Mexico and that grow today along streams and rivers but also in drier landscapes. Early evidence of cooked onions dates from 6,500 BC ("Wild Onion," n.d.). I would have used native Texas wild onions, but they are not commercially harvested and, sadly, would be difficult to source.

How to harvest and cook our native wild onions has been forgotten, the result of what Peter Kahn Jr. calls generational amnesia, the process of slowly forgetting over generations of disuse (Kahn Jr., 2002). Our ancestors baked wild onions in earth ovens and archaeological evidence shows that they were a staple food.

INGREDIENTS (SERVES 6)

- 3 lbs. leeks (they will be trimmed, deep bias)
- 1 1/2-inch piece of chile de árbol, deseeded
- 2 1/2 Tbs. dark agave nectar (not processed syrup)
- 3/4 cup apple cider vinegar
- 1/4 cup piñones (pine nuts), roasted
- 1/4 cup parsley, minced
- 1/4 cup extra virgin olive oil
- 1/4 cup tomatillo, finely minced
- 1/4 tsp. salt

METHOD

1. Trim the leeks with a sharp knife, slicing lengthwise on a steep diagonal (bias), to remove all the outer tough green leaves while preserving the tender inner greens. Slice down as far as needed, keeping intact the tender inner green leaves. Rinse the trimmed leeks thoroughly to remove grit.
2. Place the trimmed leeks in a pot, cover with water, and bring to a boil. Simmer for about 20 minutes, until you can pierce the thickest part easily with no resistance. Carefully transfer the leeks to a colander or place on paper towels to drain and cool.
3. In a saucepan, combine the agave nectar, vinegar, chile de árbol (no seeds), and salt and bring to a boil. Simmer over medium heat until the liquid is reduced by half, about 7 minutes. Remove the chile and set the mixture aside to cool.
4. In a 350°F oven, roast the piñones until they are just turning a golden brown, about 3–5 minutes. Set aside to cool.
5. Remove the papery skin and wash the tomatillo. Finely mince the tomatillo and the parsley. Set aside.
6. Whisk the agave reduction with the olive oil to emulsify, then stir in the tomatillo, piñones, and parsley until well combined.

You may keep the agave tomatillo dressing and the leeks chilled in the refrigerator for up to a couple of days. Just remember to whisk the dressing again to emulsify or shake it vigorously in a tight–lidded jar.

To serve, arrange the leeks on a serving platter with high sides and pour the tomatillo agave dressing over them, covering completely. Serve chilled or at room temperature.

Kale and red jalapeño salad (photo by author)

KALE AND RED JALAPEÑO SALAD

Kale is a nutritional superstar due to the amounts of vitamins A, B6, C, and K, folate, fiber, carotenoids, and manganese it contains. One cup of raw kale has just 20 calories (Terpstra, 2023). I did not grow up eating kale, but I'm happy that it's become trendy because it is also super healthy and delicious.

Kale is native to the Mediterranean region, and it is natural to include it as a recipe because traditionally so many Mediterranean, European, Asian, and African ingredients continued to arrive over centuries as a result of the conquest of Texas that started in 1528. In this salad, kale makes great friends with jalapeño chiles, a tasty encounter.

INGREDIENTS (MAKES 2 LARGE SALADS OR 4 SIDES)

- 4 oz. kale, washed and thinly sliced into threads
- 1 red jalapeño chile (4 Tbs.), deseeded, deveined

FOR THE DRESSING

- 3 Tbs. extra virgin olive oil
- 3 Tbs. rice vinegar
- 1 Tbs. red wine vinegar
- 1 clove garlic
- 1/4 tsp. salt
- 1/4 tsp. freshly ground black pepper
- 1 tsp. piloncillo

METHOD

1. Wash the kale and remove the spine by laying each leaf spine side up on a cutting board and slicing away each half from the spine.
2. Thinly slice the spines crosswise into small thin discs, transfer to a large bowl.
3. To slice the kale leaves, bunch together tightly a handful of the kale and then slice it very thinly with a sharp knife. There should be very thin threads. When all the kale is sliced, cut the threads crosswise into 1-inch or 1/2-inch threads. Place in the bowl with the kale discs.
4. Slice the jalapeno chile lengthwise and use a small spoon to remove the seeds and the white membranes. Then slice the chile into 1/4-inch dice. Add to the kale.
5. In a mortar, crush the garlic into a fine paste, add all the other dressing ingredients, and whisk together until emulsified. Alternately, shake the garlic paste and the other ingredients in a tightly covered bottle until emulsified.
6. Add the dressing to the kale and mix thoroughly. Taste and correct the salt. Place in the refrigerator for 30 minutes to chill.

Serve chilled.

PICKLED WATERMELON RIND AND BEAN SALAD

Watermelon (sandía) is native to Northeastern Africa where seeds have been found that date to more than 5,000 years ago. Originally a wild, sour fruit, over time a sweet version of the watermelon was domesticated for water and food there over 4,000 years ago, and by 2,000 years ago had spread throughout the Mediterranean region (Paris, 2015).

The conquest brought this dessert watermelon to Texas and Mexico where it has become a prized ingredient in Mexican gastronomy. Sandía is part of Mexican culture now, and there is even some speculation that it was the watermelon that inspired Agustín de Iturbide, a leader in Mexico's war of independence from Spain, to create the Mexican flag with the colors red, white, and green (Secretaria de Agricultura, 2016).

INGREDIENTS (SERVES 4)

- 1 small seedless watermelon
- 3 oz. tomatillos, small dice
- 1 cup red bell pepper, small dice
- 1 cup apple cider vinegar
- 3/4 cup sugar
- 1 tsp. allspice berries
- 1 star anise pod
- 15 oz. can green beans, drained
- 15 oz. can great northern beans, drained
- 1 serrano chile, stem off, sliced lengthwise in half and then sliced crosswise into half-moons
- 2 Tbs. extra virgin olive oil
- 1/2 tsp. salt
- 1/2 tsp. freshly ground black pepper

METHOD

TO PICKLE THE WATERMELON RIND

1. Cut off 1/8-inch to 1/4-inch of the outer skin of the watermelon. I do this by slicing off both ends of the watermelon (stem side and opposite) and then laying it flat on one of the cut sides. Holding the watermelon firmly, slice downward toward the middle, removing the outer skin and continuing to slice all around. Turn the watermelon over to the other flat end and do the same. The second part is to slice off the remaining white rind using the same technique. Leave about 1/4-inch of the red part on each slice. Cut the watermelon rind into 1/2-inch dice. Set aside. (Note: You will use only 4 cups of the rind for the salad, so you will not use all of the rind, depending on the size of your watermelon.)
2. In a saucepan, add the vinegar, sugar, allspice berries, and star anise and bring the mixture to a boil. Add the watermelon rind and cook on a low simmer for 15–30 minutes, until the rind is tender but not mushy.
3. Add the tomatillos and red bell pepper, then immediately remove from heat and allow to cool. Place in the refrigerator for one day and up to one week.

TO ASSEMBLE THE SALAD

In a large bowl, combine the pickled mixture, green beans, great northern beans, serrano chile, olive oil, black pepper, and salt. Taste and adjust the salt.

Serve chilled.

WATERMELON AND JÍCAMA SALAD WITH CILANTRO DRESSING

When my dad was feeling bad, he would ask for a slice of watermelon and as he tasted it, I could see the enjoyment in his face, as though his whole frame was being refreshed. This happened also with jícama. He would ask for a slice, and as he took bites, he seemed to have some deep connection, as if remembering all the times that he had enjoyed that uniquely Mexican treat. I had an uncanny sense that for him, at that moment, the embodied sense of flavor was a way of bringing in comfort and acceptance.

Two iconic ingredients, one native Mexican and the other native African, join to make a refreshing salad that I hope you will enjoy with friends.

INGREDIENTS (SERVES 6)

- 8 cups seedless watermelon, 1-inch dice
- 2 cups jícama, 1/2-inch dice
- 2 oz. cilantro stems and leaves
- 3 oz. fresh lime juice
- 1 green or dried chile piquín, stem off (2 chiles if you want more heat)
- salt to taste

METHOD

1. In a blender, place the cilantro, chile piquín, and lime juice and pulse to make a smooth dressing. Set aside.
2. In a large bowl, combine the watermelon, jicama, and cilantro-chile dressing, tossing gently to coat with the dressing. Taste and adjust the salt.

Serve chilled.

CHAPTER 4

BEANS, LENTILS, GARBANZOS

BUTTER BEANS WITH POBLANO RAJAS

This delicious combination of beans and chiles is buttery, the flavor enhanced with tomatillos and oregano. Beans and chiles simply go together so well.

Butter beans are also called lima beans and can be either green or beige in color, depending on their maturity. They are native to Guatemala, although they are named after the capital of Peru (Lima) because around AD 1700 European settlers found them there and linked them to that location (Stephens, 2018).

INGREDIENTS (SERVES 6)

- 16 oz. can butter beans
- 1 cup (4 oz.) white onion, sliced
- 1 Tbs. extra virgin olive oil
- 3 oz. tomatillos, large slices
- 1/2 Tbs. serrano chile, minced
- 2 chiles poblanos, roasted, peeled, deseeded, deveined
- 2-inch sprig fresh Texas Mexican oregano
- 1 Tbs. piloncillo
- 1/2 tsp. salt

METHOD

1. Place the poblano chiles under a broiler and cook until the skins start to blister and get slightly charred, turning them to blister on all sides, about 5 minutes per side. Remove from the broiler and cover with a damp towel for 15 minutes.
2. After 15 minutes, peel off all the skin from the chiles. Placing each on a cutting board, make a slit lengthwise, open, and remove the stem and all the seeds.
3. Lay the chiles flat on the cutting board and slice them into 2-inch x 1/4-inch strips. Set aside.
4. In a skillet, heat the olive oil on medium heat, then add the sliced onion and sauté for 5 minutes until slightly translucent and tender. Add the sliced tomatillos and oregano and cook for another 3 minutes.
5. Add the canned butter beans (including their liquid), followed by the serrano chile, poblano rajas, piloncillo, and salt. Simmer gently for 10 minutes. Taste and adjust the salt.

Serve hot.

GARBANZO, MUSHROOM, AND RED CHILE DIP

This party dip has all the inviting umami of mushrooms blended in with the garbanzo beans. Unlike other bean dips, these garbanzos are richly flavored with dried red chiles, spices, and herbs.

INGREDIENTS (MAKES 4 CUPS)

- 16 oz. can garbanzo beans
- 1 portobello mushroom (4 1/4 oz.), chopped coarsely
- corn tortillas

FOR THE CHILE PASTE (MAKES 2 CUPS)

- 8 ancho chiles
- 5 pasilla chiles
- 1 cup white vinegar
- 3 cloves garlic
- 1/2 Tbs. black peppercorns
- 1/2 tsp. ground cumin
- 3 clove buds
- 1 tsp. salt
- 1 cup water

FOR ROASTED GARLIC PASTE (MAKES 1 1/2 CUPS)

- 5 1/4 oz. garlic, peeled
- 1 4-inch sprig fresh rosemary
- 1/4 cup canola oil
- 1/2 cup white vegetable stock (p. 172)
- 1 tsp. salt
- 1 Tbs. olive oil

METHOD

1. Place all garlic paste ingredients in a saucepan and bring to a boil over medium heat. Cover tightly and transfer to a 350°F oven. Bake for 40 minutes until the garlic is very soft. Remove from oven and mash with a masher until smooth. Taste and adjust the salt as needed. Set aside.
2. In a blender, place all the chile paste ingredients and blend until completely smooth. Sift through a fine mesh sieve if there are still flecks of chile visible.
3. In a large saucepan, heat 1 Tbs. olive oil and add the chile paste. Partially cover the saucepan to catch the splatter. Cook for about 8 minutes until the paste thickens and the color deepens. Set aside to cool.
4. In a skillet, heat 1 Tbs. olive oil to the point when it becomes wavy. Add the chopped mushroom and sauté for 5 minutes or until it begins to darken in color. Set aside.
5. In a blender, place the can of garbanzo beans (with their liquid), the sautéed mushrooms, 3 Tbs. chile paste, and 3 Tbs. of the prepared garlic paste. Blend until smooth.

Serve hot with corn tortillas and serrano crudo salsa (p. 169).

Use the leftover garlic and chile for adding to cooked beans or to mashed potatoes.

Use the leftover chile paste to season mashed pinto beans when you want spicy bean tacos.

Lentejas guisadas (photo by author)

LENTEJAS GUISADAS

Lentejas guisadas are now part of our traditional cuisine, although they are native to the Mediterranean region where they began to be domesticated from 8,000 to 10,000 years ago (Liber et al., 2021). We've turned them into a true Mexican dish with ingredients of onion, tomato, and chile serrano. With the fresh cilantro added at the end for maximum flavor and aroma, it's a cousin to the famous frijoles borrachos that are boiled with beer.

INGREDIENTS (SERVES 6)

- 1 cup dry brown lentils, rinsed and drained
- 3 oz. carrot, peeled and sliced in rounds
- 2 quarts water
- 2 Tbs. canola or other vegetable oil
- 1 medium white onion, small dice
- 1 clove garlic, minced
- 8 oz. ripe tomatoes, coarsely chopped
- 1 serrano chile, whole, stem removed
- 3 Tbs. cilantro, coarsely chopped
- 2 thin, round slices of white onion
- 1/2 tsp. salt

METHOD

1. In a large saucepan, cover the lentils with 2 quarts of water and bring to a boil. Reduce the heat and simmer for 30–45 minutes until the lentils are soft and soupy.
2. In a skillet, heat the oil over medium heat and sauté the onion until translucent, about 5 minutes. Add the garlic and cook for 1 minute longer. Add the tomatoes and continue cooking until most of the liquid has evaporated, stirring as needed.
3. Add the tomato mixture, carrots, salt, and serrano chile to the lentils and simmer for 10 minutes.
4. Add the cilantro, stir, and add salt as desired.

Serve in bowls and garnish with the sliced onions.

The lentejas can be made several hours ahead of time (without adding the cilantro), kept in the refrigerator, and then reheated, adding the fresh cilantro just before serving.

LENTILS WITH SWISS CHARD | LENTEJAS Y ACELGA

As I was growing up, our family always ate greens during the growing season, Swiss chard among them. My amá, Dominga Mora Medrano, would wash the greens thoroughly and then boil them or make them into a guisado with onions. This combination with lentils makes a delightful full meal.

Swiss chard is not from Switzerland but from the Mediterranean region, cultivated over 2,000 years ago. Acelgas are known to decrease the risk of obesity, diabetes, and heart disease. They are packed with antioxidants and contain high levels of vitamins K, A, and C, magnesium, potassium, iron, and fiber. Eating plenty of chard can help maintain bone health, improve digestion, regulate blood sugar levels, and contribute to healthy brain function (Mahr, n.d.).

INGREDIENTS (SERVES 6)

- 8 oz. raw lentils, rinsed and drained
- 2 cloves garlic, minced
- 4 cups water
- 2 oz. green bulb onions
- 11 oz. Swiss chard, any variety, washed
- 1 Tbs. extra virgin olive oil
- 1 tsp. salt
- corn tortillas

METHOD

1. In a saucepan, boil the lentils and 1 minced garlic clove in 4 cups of water for 30 minutes, until they are cooked and tender.
2. Slice the onion bulb and the entire green stems crosswise. Set aside.
3. Using a paring knife, remove the large stalks from the center of each Swiss chard leaf, then slice the stalks crosswise into 1/4-inch pieces. Tear or slice the leaves into pieces that are about 4 inches long. Set the leaves and stalk aside.
4. In a skillet, heat 1 Tbs. olive oil, then add the green onion, the Swiss chard stalks, and 1 minced garlic clove. Sauté for 5 minutes, until the onion bulbs become translucent.
5. When the lentils are cooked, add the onion mixture, the Swiss chard leaves, and 1 tsp. salt, and let simmer for 5–7 minutes, until the leaves are cooked.

Serve hot with corn tortillas.

TOKSEL

Toksel is delicious and super nutritious. Besides the nutritional values of the lima beans, pepitas are rich in magnesium and omega 3 acids and high in fiber all of which helps maintain cardiovascular health (Espinosa, 2018).

I include Toksel, a traditional dish from far south in the Mayan region of Mesoamerica, because it is another strong example of the cosmopolitan character of Texas Mexican peoples. Toksel combines lima beans, native to Guatemala, with seeds from squash, which is native to South Texas and Northeastern Mexico.

Beautiful dishes like this one were the result of constant travel and food exchanges among Mayan, Coahuiltecan, Apache, and other civilizations of North and Central America. Pepitas from Texas reached the Aztecs and became part of their cuisine before the arrival of the Spanish conquerors. The Spanish priest, Fray Bernardino de Sahagún, describes various dishes made with squash seeds (pepitas), including grinding them and mixing with red chile and tomatoes. He also reports their use as a food in ceremonial settings (Sahagún, 1540).

INGREDIENTS (SERVES 6)

- 1/2 lb. frozen lima beans
- 3 oz. green onion
- 6 oz. hulled pumpkin seeds, roasted
- 1 Tbs. canola oil
- 1/2 tsp. salt or to taste
- 1 lime (juice)

METHOD

1. Roast the hulled pumpkin seeds in a cast iron or other skillet over medium heat for about 5 minutes or until they start to turn golden in color. Remove immediately from the heat so that they do not burn. Set aside to cool, then place them in a blender, spice grinder, or molcajete and crush them coarsely. Set aside.
2. In a saucepan, cover the frozen lima beans with water and boil for 13 minutes, until they are cooked. Drain and set aside.
3. In a skillet, heat the oil over medium heat, then add the lima beans and cook them so that they begin to acquire a golden color, about 3 minutes. Add the green onion, pumpkin seeds, and salt and cook for a minute longer, then lower the heat to low, cover, and cook for an additional 5 minutes. Remove from the heat and add the lime juice and mix well.

Serve immediately with corn tortillas and a tomato-based salsa like chile piquín salsa.

CHAPTER 5

GUISADOS Y SALTEADOS | STEWS AND SAUTÉES

2G

CALABACITA SALTEADA

The trick to this straightforward technique is to cook the squash half-moons just enough so that they begin to get tender, then stop the heat. You'll be able to bite into the calabacitas because they will remain slightly firm. Make tacos with corn tortillas, topped with chile ancho en escabeche (p. 160).

INGREDIENTS (SERVES 4)

- 1 lb. Mexican calabacita or zucchini
- 1 Tbs. extra virgin olive oil
- salt to taste

METHOD

1. Wash the zucchini. Cut off the ends and slice in half, lengthwise. Slice each half crosswise to form 1/2-inch-thick half-moons.
2. In a 12-inch skillet, heat the oil over medium heat. When the oil starts to shimmer (make little waves) add the calabacita and sauté for about 10 minutes, until the half-moons are tender but still maintain their firm shape. Overcooking will render them mushy.
3. Taste and add salt as needed.

CALABACITAS CON ACHIOTE

Achiote is a common spice in the Yucatán and comes from the seeds of the annatto tree. I've noticed that it has become more used in Texas, both in powder and paste form, as kitchens integrate it into local dishes to create delicious new flavors.

In this recipe achiote infuses tatuma or zucchini squash with a peppery sweet flavor. It also adds a distinctive deep yellow-orange color. (Actually, you can boil a cup of the powder in a pot of water and then dye a white shirt, blouse, or skirt with that same beautiful yellow-orange hue.)

INGREDIENTS (SERVES 4)

- 1 1/2 lbs. Mexican tatuma squashes (or substitute zucchini)
- 2 1/2 Tbs. achiote paste
- 1 tsp. black peppercorns
- 1 tsp. dried Mexican oregano
- 2 cloves garlic
- 2 Tbs. vegetable oil
- 1 1/2 cups water
- 1 1/2 tsp. salt

METHOD

1. Cut the squash into 1-inch dice; set aside.
2. In a molcajete or other mortar, mash the garlic with the black peppercorns to make a smooth paste. Add the achiote paste and combine.
3. In a saucepan, over medium heat, add 1 1/2 cups water and achiote paste and bring to a boil. Simmer slowly for 10 minutes.
4. Add the squash, oregano, salt, and oil and bring back up to a simmer. Lower the heat and cook, uncovered, for 5 minutes or until the squash is cooked tender but still firm, not mushy.

Serve immediately, or cool and store in the refrigerator for up to two days.

SAUTÉED CHAYOTE

Chayote is called mirliton in Louisiana where it is used in Cajun cooking, but it is one of the most recognized and typical Mexican culinary ingredients. Originally from the area of Mexico and Guatemala, it is believed to have been cultivated in the year 1200 BC (Pu et al., 2021), so it is an ancient and delicious ingredient in Mexican gastronomy.

You may want to make this sauté as an everyday taco filling and then finish with serrano crudo salsa (p. 169) or serve it with a generous portion of pecan and mesquite mole (p. 48).

INGREDIENTS (SERVES 4)

- 2 chayotes
- 1 Tbs. garlic, minced
- 1 Tbs. canola oil or other vegetable oil
- 1/8 tsp. Mexican oregano
- 1/2 tsp. salt
- 1/4 tsp. black pepper

METHOD

1. In a saucepan, place the chayote and add water to cover the chayote by 2 inches. Bring to a boil, then reduce the heat and simmer for 55 minutes. Pierce with a fork to make sure it is cooked and tender. Remove the chayote and when it is cool enough to handle, peel it, cut it in half, remove the seed, then cut it lengthwise into 1/4-inch-thick slices. Then cut each slice, lengthwise again, to make little sticks that are 1/4-inch by 1/4-inch thick.
2. In a skillet, heat the oil over medium heat. Add the garlic and swirl it for a mere 30 seconds. Add the chayote, oregano, salt, and black pepper and heat it through.

Serve immediately.

CHILES TOREADOS

Chiles take center stage in this traditional cooking method. Chiles serranos are cooked whole, so they will be hot and with those unmistakable serrano herbal notes. The chiles jalapeños are for guests who prefer less heat, so they are deseeded, with the white membranes removed.

The Spanish word, toreado, refers to bullfighting and specifically to the bull that's taunted in a bullfight. Bite into these chiles that have been turned and tossed around in hot oil and you'll see the meaning of chile toreado.

The Texas Mexican region has the honor of being one of two ancient sites for the original culinary use of chiles. Romero's Cave in the state of Tamaulipas (think near Brownsville, Harlingen, McAllen) is the site of archaeological evidence indicating the birthplace of our chile, 7,000 to 9,000 years ago. The other site is a cave in the Tehuacán valley of the state of Puebla (Kraft et al., 2014).

When making this delicious recipe, then, take a moment and think about the hundreds and thousands of years that people before you have domesticated and enjoyed the delicious flavor of chiles.

INGREDIENTS (SERVES 8)

- 3 serrano chiles, washed, dried, stem on
- 3 jalapeño chiles, washed and dried, with stems, seeds, and white membranes removed, quartered lengthwise
- 1 cup white onion, sliced
- 2 Tbs. extra virgin olive oil
- juice of 1 lime (optional)
- 1/2 tsp. salt

METHOD

1. In a large skillet, heat the olive oil over medium-low heat. Add the jalapeño and serrano chiles and the salt and cook for 7–10 minutes. Use tongs to turn the chiles so they cook evenly.
2. When the chiles begin to blister, add the sliced onions and combine well. Cook for an additional 3–5 minutes, until the onions are translucent and have begun to acquire color.
3. Add the lime juice, if using, and mix well.

Serve hot or at room temperature. Use on mushroom tacos (p. 36) or with any other tacos or dishes as a garnish and condiment.

Colache de calabacitas (photo by author)

COLACHE DE CALABACITAS

Colache is a salteado dish from the state of Sinaloa in Northwest Mexico, home of the Yaqui people. The main ingredient traditionally is the heirloom tatuma squash, but zucchini is a good substitute. It can have a variety of additional ingredients, including green beans and corn. This recipe emphasizes the straightforward flavor of the calabacita paired with the roasted chiles poblanos.

INGREDIENTS (SERVES 4)

- 3 poblano chiles
- 1 3/4 lbs. Mexican calabacita or tatuma squash or zucchini (6 cups diced)
- 3 Tbs. white onion, diced small
- 1/2 tsp. garlic, minced
- 1/2 tsp. sugar
- 1 tsp. salt
- ground black pepper, to taste

METHOD

1. Place the poblano chiles under a broiler and cook them for about 5–7 minutes, until the skin blisters, turning slightly brown with some black spots. Flip them and do the same to the other side. Remove them from the broiler and cover completely with a damp cloth for 15 minutes.
2. When cool enough to handle, peel the outer paper-thin skin from the chiles. Slice each chile lengthwise to remove all the seeds and the stem. Slice the chiles into rajas (strips) that are 1/4-inch wide by 2 inches long. Set aside.
3. In a saucepan filled with boiling water, place the diced squash and blanche for 2 minutes. Drain, and then return the squash to the saucepan (no oil nor water) and add the onion, garlic, sugar, salt, and black pepper. Stir the ingredients together, then add the poblano rajas. Cover and cook on low heat until the colache is heated through.

Serve immediately.

FLOR DE JAMAICA EN CHILE COLORADO

Although mainly known for brewing the iconic agua de Jamaica, hibiscus flowers make delicious savory entrées when used for enchiladas, tacos, and stews. The origin of the hibiscus flower is placed in three possible regions, India, Saudi Arabia, and Western Sudan in Africa, where evidence is found dating domestication of hibiscus to 4000 BC (Da-Costa-Rocha et al., 2014). It arrived in Mexico with colonization and has become integrated into the fabric of Mexican cuisine.

This is a versatile recipe that can be taken as a casserole dish for a potluck gathering or for an innovative filling for taco Tuesdays.

INGREDIENTS (MAKES 7–8 CUPS)

- 2 cups boiled and drained hibiscus flowers
- 4 chiles guajillos
- 3 Roma tomatoes
- small white onion, 5 oz., peeled
- 1/4 cup carrot, peeled and shredded
- 1 clove garlic, unpeeled
- 1 tsp. fresh Mexican oregano
- 5 allspice berries
- 1/2 tsp. ground cumin
- 1/2 tsp. salt
- 1 Tbs. canola oil
- 1/2 to 1 cup water as needed to blend
- 4 cups water

METHOD

1. Deseed and devein the chile guajillo, then place it in a saucepan with enough water to cover them. Cover the saucepan and bring to a boil; turn off the heat, and hold covered for 20 minutes to rehydrate.
2. Heat a comal (griddle) or cast iron skillet over medium heat and add the tomato, peeled onion, and unpeeled garlic, turning them as needed. Dry roast for 5 to 10 minutes until the vegetables have softened and acquired black spots. Set aside.
3. On a cutting board, finely mince the hibiscus flowers and set aside.
4. In a blender, add the dehydrated chiles, tomatoes, onion, garlic, oregano, allspice, ground cumin, and salt plus 1/2 to 1 cup water as needed. Blend for about 90 seconds to make a smooth purée.
5. In a large saucepan or Dutch oven, heat 1 Tbs. canola oil, then add the chile purée. Watch out for splatter. Cook for 8 to 10 minutes until the color has deepened and the purée has thickened.
6. Add the hibiscus flowers, the shredded carrots, and 4 cups of water to the chile purée. Bring to a boil and simmer, uncovered, for 45 minutes. Correct the salt.

Garnish with peeled, sliced arracacha, if you can find it at a Latinx market. It's a white carrot with a nutty flavor, somewhat resembling a parsnip. This blend also makes an excellent taco, garnished with pickled jalapeño slices.

2G

TUPINAMBO SALTEADO | SAUTÉED JERUSALEM ARTICHOKES

Jerusalem artichokes, also called sunchokes, are the tubers of the sunflower, *Helianthus tuberosus*. It was an everyday food of our ancestors living in South Texas and Northeastern Mexico but has since been forgotten and fallen into disuse. By reclaiming this food tradition, we can also reclaim a path to health because sunchokes are high in protein and are a good source of minerals, vitamins, and even electrolytes.

This basic sauté will open up the flavor so that you can mix it with other vegetables and also dress it with chile serrano vinaigrette (p. 163).

INGREDIENTS (SERVES 4)

- 1/2 lb. Jerusalem artichokes
- 1 Tbs. canola oil
- 1 cup water
- salt to taste

METHOD

1. Wash the Jerusalem artichokes very well, making sure to remove all the dirt in the crevices of the little tubers. Brush lightly to remove some of the dark skin, then cut them into 1/4-inch slices.
2. Place the sliced Jerusalem artichokes in a 10-inch or 12-inch skillet. Add water and canola oil. Bring to a boil, then turn down the heat and simmer, uncovered, for 15 minutes until the water has evaporated. Scrape the pan to toss the Jerusalem artichokes so they cook evenly. Pierce with a fork to test that they are tender. Taste and add salt as needed.

MUSHROOMS WITH CALABACITA AND CORN

Calabacita with corn is a traditional guisado, and here it is given an umami lift with cremini mushrooms and brightness with my favorite chile, the serrano. Mushrooms do not represent a steady food source of Texas Indians, but there is some evidence that suggests that they did eat fungus growing on certain decomposing materials ("J. B. White Daily Life," n.d.). Be that as it may, this is only one of many recipes that make Texas Mexican plant-based cooking imaginative and tasty.

INGREDIENTS (SERVES 6)

- 1 lb. cremini mushrooms, sliced
- 1 lb. Mexican calabacita or zucchini, cut into 1/2-inch dice
- 1 cup corn kernels
- 4 oz. scallions (about 2 large), sliced crosswise into thin rounds
- 1 clove garlic, minced
- 1 serrano chile, sliced thinly lengthwise, cut into 1-inch sticks
- 4 Tbs. extra virgin olive oil
- 1/2 tsp. salt
- 3 epazote leaves, coarsely chopped

METHOD

In a large skillet, heat the extra virgin olive oil over medium heat, then add the scallions and cook for 2 minutes. Add the minced garlic and cook for another 30 seconds. Add the mushrooms, calabacita, corn, serrano chile, and salt and cook for 5 minutes, stirring as needed. To increase moisture, cover the skillet and cook for another 2 minutes. The ingredients should be moist. Add 1/4 cup of water if deglazing the pan is needed.

Add the chopped epazote leaves and serve immediately.

Mushrooms with calabacita and corn (photo by author)

NOPALITOS WITH RED CHILE

Nopalitos and red chiles are a flavor binary—that is, two ingredients whose flavors are so delicious together, it seems that nature always intended them to be eaten together as one memorable flavor. I like to enjoy this flavor binary as is, with corn tortillas, but you can also take binaries and mix and expand them into more complex flavors with spices and herbs.

In almost all nopalitos recipes the chiles are mixed with garlic. In the South Texas region, we also add cumin but farther south, into Central and Southern Mexico, they don't like cumin and add oregano instead. Enjoy these red chile nopalitos on a plate with boiled pinto beans and corn tortillas.

INGREDIENTS (SERVES 6)

FOR THE NOPALITOS

- 3 cups fresh nopales (cactus paddles), 1/2-inch squares
- 3/4 cup white onion, small dice
- 1/2 tsp. salt or to taste
- 1/2 cup water
- 1 Tbs. canola oil or other vegetable oil
- 1/2 cup cilantro leaves, coarsely chopped, for garnish (optional)
- 1/4 lb. queso de almendras (p. 159) for garnish (optional)

FOR THE CHILE PASTE

- 1 garlic clove
- 3 ancho chiles, cleaned, seeded, and deveined
- 3 guajillo chiles, cleaned, seeded, and deveined
- 1/2 tsp. ground cumin
- 3/4 cup water
- 2 Tbs. canola oil or other vegetable oil
- 1 tsp. salt or to taste

METHOD

FOR THE CHILE PASTE

1. To devein the chiles, first lay the chile flat on a cutting board and, using a paring knife, cut a slit lengthwise. Grab the chile with one hand and with the other remove the stem along with the bunch of seeds still attached to it. Open the chile along the slit and remove the remaining seeds and veins.
2. In a large saucepan, cover the cleaned chiles with water and bring to a boil. Turn off the heat and let the chiles steep for 15 minutes so that they rehydrate and become tender.
3. Drain the chiles. Let the chiles cool a bit and then place in a blender along with the garlic, cumin, and salt. Blend to a very fine paste, adding 1/2–1 cup water as needed.
4. In a saucepan, heat 1 Tbs. canola oil and add the chile paste from the blender. It will splatter, so take care. Cook for 8–10 minutes until the color deepens and the paste thickens. Set aside.

TO COOK THE NOPALITOS

1. To remove the spines from the cactus, first cover your working surface with paper. Hold the cactus paddle with tongs and use a sharp knife or a potato peeler to slice

around the edge of the cactus, removing all the spines on the edges, then lay the paddle flat and scrape off the rest. Remove only the little bumps where the spines are growing. The other parts of the cactus paddle will remain unpeeled. When finished, roll up the newspaper carefully and discard.

2. Rinse the cactus paddles, then slice them into 1/2-inch squares.
3. Heat 1 Tbs. canola or other vegetable oil in a skillet on medium heat and cook the cactus squares for 13–15 minutes. Add the onion and cook 2 minutes, stirring. Add 3/4 cup chile paste and 1/2 cup water and combine well. Cover and cook on low for 5 minutes. Add more water if the chile is too thick. Adjust the salt.

Serve hot with corn tortillas. Garnish with cilantro and queso de almendras (p. 159), if using, and chile piquín salsa (optional, p. 168).

TURNIP AND AMARANTH IN TOMATILLO SAUCE

The leaves of the red root amaranth plant, *Amaranthus retroflexus*, are rich in calcium, iron, and folic acid and were a staple food for the Native people of Texas. Our ancestors cooked many species of amaranth, most commonly by steaming or boiling the leaves of young plants, and sometimes the entire plant ("Nature-Amaranth," n.d.). In this recipe the delicious flavor of the leaves is combined with cubes of turnip for a hearty meal.

When I was growing up, my mom would take me along to forage for amaranth in the wild fields, and we called the greens quelitre. It was a constant part of our diet, but over time it became less so, and now this new generation has forgotten it. It is yet another example of our healthful and traditional foods suffering the effects of generational amnesia (Kahn Jr., 2002).

As I explained in my previous book, *Truly Texas Mexican: A Native Culinary Heritage in Recipes*, the plural word, quelites, is used in Southern Mexico to denote a whole array of plants with green leaves that are suitable for cooking. Our Texas *Amaranthus retroflexus* would be considered one quelite among many other different types of quelites. "Quilitl" is the Nahuatl word meaning edible greens. But in my family and community, quelitre, with an "r," refers to the specific plant that's used in this recipe, *Amaranthus retroflexus* (Medrano, 2014).

INGREDIENTS (SERVES 4)

- 12 oz. turnips, peeled, medium dice
- 2 oz. (4 cups) red-root amaranth leaves
- 5 1/4 oz. tomatillos, peeled, washed, and quartered
- 1 clove garlic
- 1/4 cup onion
- 1 Tbs. extra virgin olive oil
- 1/2 tsp. salt
- 2 tsp. sugar

METHOD

1. In a large saucepan, place the red-root amaranth and cover with water 2 inches above the leaves. Cover and bring the water to a boil. Reduce the heat and simmer for 20 minutes.
2. Add the diced turnip, cover, and simmer for another 20 minutes or until the turnip is cooked and soft.
3. In a blender, place the tomatillos, garlic, onion, salt, and sugar and blend to make a smooth purée.
4. In a small saucepan, heat the olive oil, then pour in the tomatillo purée. Bring the mixture to a boil, then simmer for 12 minutes. The color will deepen. Set aside.
5. When the turnips are cooked, drain them, together with the amaranth. Transfer to a large bowl, add the tomatillo sauce, and mix gently to combine. Taste and adjust the salt.

Serve hot.

Turnip and amaranth in tomatillo sauce (photo by author)

MASHED TURNIP WITH POBLANO RAJAS

Turnips are an ancient root from the middle and East Asian region. We ate them regularly at home because my father's business was buying crops of vegetables from South Texas farmers and taking them to market. As a teenager, I used to work in the fields, picking the turnips, then washing them and stringing them together into bunches. I'd sit at the back of the truck, selling them to grocery store owners and other retailers who travelled to the San Antonio wholesale produce market, an expansive concrete and stucco warehouse.

It was called the Farmers Market, on West Commerce Street, and was built in 1938. It was closed in the late 1960s and turned into an immense curio shop that today underpins the city center as a tourist magnet. My dad was upset when the farmers market morphed into a tourist location, wrecking the occupations of many local Mexican American entrepreneurs who had developed business relationships with farmers in the region. It was one of the first casualties as big business and corporations began to take over the delivery of fresh produce to homes. All of these memories surface every time I cook turnips. Then I concentrate on the delicious flavors of this underappreciated root vegetable.

Turnips get a boost of creaminess from cashews in this recipe. The poblano rajas add great flavor but also color and texture to the mash.

INGREDIENTS (SERVES 6)

- 3 large turnips, peeled, quartered
- 3 chiles poblanos, fresh
- 4 Tbs. roasted cashews
- 3 cups sliced yellow onion
- 1 Tbs. extra virgin olive oil
- 1/2 cup water
- salt to taste

METHOD

Preheat oven to 350°F

1. Cover the cashews with 1/2 cup water and allow to soak for 4 hours or overnight. (You can skip this step if you're short on time, or use boiling water and let them soak for 30 minutes or as long as possible.) Soaking the cashews encourages creaminess.
2. In a skillet, heat 1 Tbs. extra virgin olive oil and add the sliced onions. Cook over low heat until the onions are soft and translucent, about 5–7 minutes. Keep the heat on low so that the onions don't brown. Set aside.
3. Place the peeled and quartered turnips in a large saucepan, cover them with water, and bring to a boil. After the water starts to boil, cook them for 15 minutes or until they are completely tender. Drain them and set aside.
4. Place the chiles under a broiler and cook until the skins blister and get slightly

charred, turning them to broil on all sides, about 5 minutes per side. Remove from the broiler and cover with a damp towel for 15 minutes.

5. After 15 minutes, peel off all the skin from the chiles. Placing each on a cutting board, make a slit lengthwise, open, and remove all the seeds.
6. Lay the chiles flat on the cutting board and slice them into 3-inch x 3/4-inch strips. Set aside.
7. In a food processor, place the cashews and 1/4 of the turnips and process until the cashews and purée are completely smooth, with no graininess. Add the remainder of the turnips and process until the purée is smooth.
8. In a large bowl, combine the purée with the poblano rajas, sliced onions, and salt until the mixture is thoroughly combined.
9. Transfer the mixture to a baking dish, cover tightly, and bake in the oven for 40 minutes so that the flavors combine.

Serve hot.

FEATURED Today
$2 99

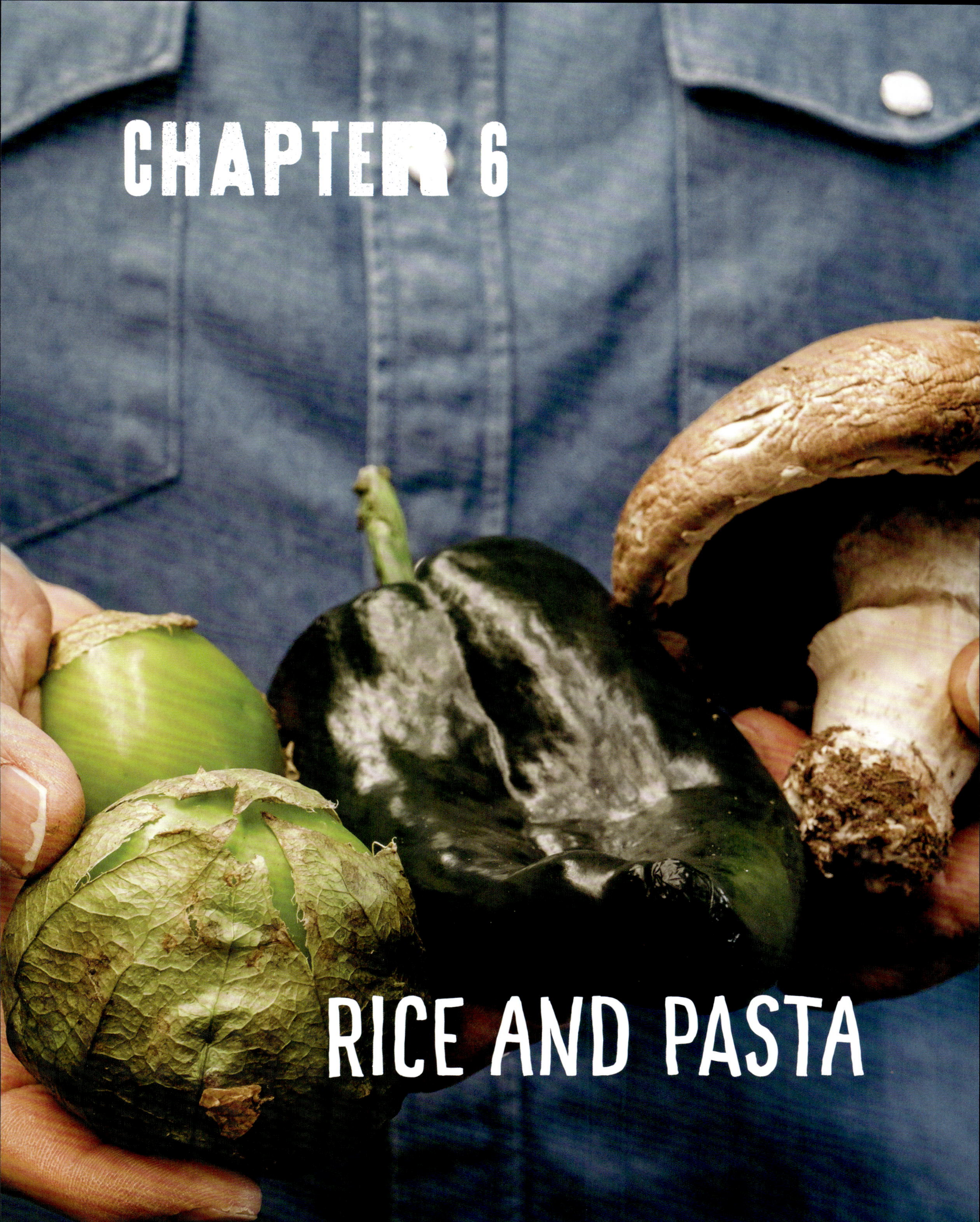

CHAPTER 6

RICE AND PASTA

CHILE POBLANO RICE

Roasted poblano chiles perk up whole grain brown rice, flavored with a touch of Texas Mexican oregano. Of the two types of oregano that are called Mexican, the one I recommend for this recipe is *Poliomintha longiflora*. It is native to Texas and the Mexican northern states of Nuevo León, Coahuila, and San Luis Potosí. It's a member of the mint family and blooms with tiny lavender or pink flowers. At the nursery it may be called rosemary mint.

The flavor of Texas Mexican oregano is milder and brighter than the more widely used Mexican oregano, *Lippia graveolens*, which is a member of the verbena herb family (Medrano, 2014). The latter is the default oregano for Central and Southern Mexico dishes and is what is sold in grocery stores. Texas Mexican oregano is not sold in stores, but you can buy it online or plant some in your yard. It's a perennial bush that grows easily and loves the heat. You'll love the flavor it adds to this dish.

INGREDIENTS (MAKES 2 CUPS)

- 1/2 cup onion, diced
- 1 Tbs. extra virgin olive oil
- 1 cup brown rice
- 1 chile poblano, roasted, deseeded, deveined
- 1/2 tsp. Texas Mexican oregano
- 1/2 tsp. salt
- 2 cups white vegetable stock (p. 172)
- 2 Tbs. parsley, coarsely chopped

METHOD

1. Place the chile poblano under a broiler and cook it for about 5 minutes, until the skin blisters, turning slightly brown with some black spots. Flip it and do the same to the other side. Remove it from the broiler and cover completely with a damp cloth for 15 minutes.
2. When cool enough to handle, peel the outer paper-thin skin from the chile. Make a slit in the chile, lengthwise, to open it and remove all the seeds and the stem. Cut the chile lengthwise into 1/4-inch strips, then slice the strips crosswise to make 1/4-inch squares. Set aside.
3. In a blender, add 1 cup white vegetable stock, parsley, and oregano. Blend until the herbs have liquified and the stock is slightly green. Set aside.
4. In a medium saucepan, heat the olive oil over medium heat, then add the rice and cook for 2 minutes, until it begins to darken in color. Add the onion and cook an additional 3 minutes. The onion will become translucent and the rice will darken more in color.
5. Add the blender liquid, diced poblano chile, salt, and the additional cup of stock. Bring to a boil, then turn down the heat to low, cover, and cook for 35–40 minutes, until the rice is cooked, tender but not mushy.

CONCHITAS | SHELL PASTA

Every Texas Mexican American family knows and loves this dish. It's one of two iconic pasta dishes, the other one being fideo. If conchitas could talk, the entire social, cultural, feminist, civil rights history of the Mexican American community would be told. Actually, in the making of conchitas today we do retell our journey.

When making conchitas I remember my childhood, and it identifies who I am and where I come from. I'm elated to be able to include this dish, a prime example of plant-based traditions that have sustained us and will continue to do so into the future we are making.

INGREDIENTS (SERVES 4)

- 12 oz. conchitas (shell-shaped pasta)
- 20 oz. Roma tomatoes, diced
- 8 oz. white onion, small dice
- 4 cloves garlic, minced
- 2 Tbs. canola oil
- 2 tsp. salt
- 1 tsp. freshly ground black pepper
- 1 quart water

METHOD

1. In a large skillet, heat the oil on high heat, then add the conchitas and the onion and cook for 5 minutes, stirring so as not to burn.
2. Add the garlic and tomato and cook for 1 minute.
3. Add the water, salt, and black pepper. Bring to a boil, then reduce the heat to medium and simmer, uncovered, for 20 minutes, until the conchitas are cooked and most, not all, of the water has evaporated.

Serve immediately. The conchitas can be cooled for serving later and reheated on the stove top very slowly over low heat until heated through.

MUSHROOM AND GREEN OLIVE RICE

This is a guisado to comfort the whole extended family, so double or triple the recipe. With the addition of the briny green olives, it echoes the fricasés of the Caribbean countries, but it sticks to this region because of the unique Texas Mexican trinity of spices: ajo, comino, pimiento (garlic, cumin, black pepper). This trio is unique to the region of South Texas and Northeastern Mexico, and the flavor combination is found in many traditional dishes, including tamales and enchiladas.

INGREDIENTS (SERVES 4)

- 1 lb. oyster mushrooms
- 1 cup brown rice
- 1 large ripe tomato (8 oz.), diced
- 1/2 small white onion, diced
- 1/2 cup pimiento-stuffed green olives
- 1 clove garlic
- 1/2 tsp. black peppercorns
- 1/2 tsp. cumin
- 1/2 tsp. salt
- 2 Tbs. extra virgin olive oil
- 2 cups water

METHOD

1. Wash all the dirt off the oyster mushrooms with cold water, then dry them using a salad spinner. Slice them lengthwise into 1/4-inch strips, then slice them crosswise into 1-inch strips. Set aside.
2. In a molcajete or other mortar, crush the garlic, cumin, black peppercorns, and salt until the mixture is a smooth paste. Set aside.
3. In a large saucepan, heat 1 Tbs. extra virgin olive oil until it begins to shimmer on the surface but before it smokes. Add the oyster mushrooms and cook them for 5 minutes, stirring, until golden brown. Transfer to a plate.
4. In a large saucepan, heat 1 Tbs. extra virgin olive oil and when it begins to shimmer, add the rice and cook for 1 minute, stirring. Add the onion and cook for 1 minute. Add the tomato and cook for another minute. Add the mushrooms, then the pimiento-stuffed green olives.
5. Measure 2 cups of water and add some of it to the molcajete or mortar to release the spice paste, then add it to the rice. Add the remaining water and bring to a simmer. Cover and reduce the heat to very low and cook for 40–45 minutes until the rice is cooked, tender but not mushy.

Serve the rice with a green vegetable like boiled ejote (green beans).

MUSHROOM PAELLA

Spanish cuisine came to Texas a few decades after about 80 would-be conquerors shipwrecked off the coast of Galveston Island in 1528. It was in the late 1600s that Spanish expeditions began to settle Texas and Northeastern Mexico. In 1689 and 1690, Alonso de León led two expeditions from 35 miles below Eagle Pass to beyond the Brazos River. He arrived with food products like wheat and beef, and these eventually became part of our indigenous foodways (Montaño, 2023).

Paella is one of the traditional Spanish dishes that caught on, over time, and today it is celebrated in Texas with festivals and cook-offs. This recipe is a plant cornucopia with the heady aroma of saffron, and making it is a real fiesta.

INGREDIENTS (SERVES 4)

- 2 cups brown arborio rice, if available. Otherwise use white. (Brown rice will take longer to cook than white arborio rice, but the flavor and nutrition are superlative.)
- 11 oz. (2 cups) sliced white onion
- 5 oz. red bell pepper, sliced into 3-inch by 1/4-inch strips
- 2 stalks celery, thinly sliced crosswise
- 1 cup sliced water chestnuts
- 1 cup green peas, fresh or frozen
- 1 cup large black olives, sliced into halves
- 1 lb. oyster mushrooms, cut into 1-inch and 2-inch pieces
- 1 tsp. black pepper
- 1 1/2 tsp. salt
- 1 1/2 cups dry white wine
- 1 tsp. saffron
- 4 cups water, warm
- 4 Tbs. extra virgin olive oil
- lemon slices for garnish

METHOD

1. Place the saffron in 4 cups warm water, along with the salt, and set aside.
2. In a large skillet, heat 2 Tbs. olive oil to the point that it begins to show waves, then add the oyster mushrooms and sauté until they begin to turn golden in color and a bit crispy on the edges, about 5–6 minutes. Set aside.
3. In a large paella pan or skillet, heat 2 Tbs. olive oil over medium heat, then add the onion, red bell pepper, and celery and sauté until they soften and begin to get some color, about 10 minutes.
4. Add the white wine to the vegetables and scrape to deglaze, removing all the particles that have stuck to the pan.
5. When the wine is almost evaporated, add the rice, oyster mushrooms, water chestnuts, black pepper, and saffron water. Stir to combine completely. Cover and cook on a low simmer for 45 minutes.
6. After 45 minutes, uncover the pan. The brown rice should still be a little hard. Add the peas and black olives and gently combine. Do not scrape the bottom of the pan. There's a crust layer forming that will be delicious. Add a little more water if it looks too dry. Cover and cook for another 15 minutes or until the rice is completely cooked.

Serve immediately, garnished with lemon slices.

Mushroom paella (photo by author)

CHAPTER 7

CONDIMENTS

CHILE DULCE | BELL PEPPER SALSA

Moscow was where I debuted this green salsa, for a garden gala at the residence of the US ambassador to Russia. Ambassador Jon Huntsman invited me to be the featured chef at the official Fourth of July celebration, a grand social occasion among business and prominent Russians. However, I'd run into a snag.

My menu included flour tacos with a green salsa, but I had been told that there were no tomatillos to be found in the Moscow markets. So I began testing alternatives in my Houston test kitchen and found that green bell peppers work very well once they have been deseeded and boiled for an hour. Boiling removes the bitterness, turning them into a base of tangy green flavor. With serrano chiles, onion, and garlic, I had our green salsa for Moscow. It was a hit.

I hope you will enjoy this salsa on your tacos and dishes as much as our guests and friends in Moscow did.

INGREDIENTS (MAKES 1 1/2 CUPS)

- 2 green bell peppers (chile dulce)
- 1/4 small onion
- 2 cloves garlic, unpeeled
- 1 tsp. white distilled white vinegar
- 1 Tbs. lemon juice
- 1 tsp. salt or to taste
- 1/2 tsp. minced jalapeños (add more, 1/2 tsp. at a time, if you want more jalapeño flavor and heat)

METHOD

1. Remove the outer stem from the bell peppers, and slice them in half and remove the seeds. Place them in a saucepan, cover with water, bring to a boil, then lower the heat and simmer for 1 hour. This extended cooking time decreases the bitterness.
2. During the last 30 minutes of simmering, add the onion and garlic cloves. Drain onto a colander and allow to cool. Peel the garlic.
3. Place the chile dulce (green bell peppers), onion, and garlic in a blender and add the vinegar, lemon juice, jalapeño, and salt and blend until smooth. Taste the level of heat; if you want it stronger, keep adding more minced jalapeños 1/2 tsp. at a time.

Taste and adjust the salt. I love this salsa on grilled veggie tacos, served either hot or at room temperature.

CEBOLLAS ENCURTIDAS

Flavors like this, with orange juice and chile habanero, are not native to South Texas and Northeastern Mexico but originate in the south of Mexico, in the Yucatán region. More and more, though, I'm starting to use these cebollas encurtidas for all types of dishes, like garnish for enchiladas and toppings for some vegetables.

INGREDIENTS (MAKES 1 CUP)

- 1 red onion
- 1/2 cup orange juice
- 1/2 cup lime juice
- 2 Tbs. apple cider vinegar
- 1/2 habanero chile, minced
- 1/2 tsp. dried Mexican oregano
- salt to taste

METHOD

1. Cut the onion in half and slice it thinly, crosswise, forming half circles.
2. In a pot of boiling water, blanche the onion for 1 minute; drain.
3. Place the onions and all the other ingredients in a glass container and marinate for at least 3 hours, preferably overnight.

Brighten your tacos with these zesty onions or serve them as garnish for calabacitas (p. 120) or sautéed chayote (p. 123).

CHAMOY CASERO

The origins of chamoy as a dried fruit condiment are obscure, but the consensus is that they are Asian, either Japanese or Chinese. Once it reached Mexico, of course, it was transformed with chiles and now it is a delicious iconic staple.

INGREDIENTS (MAKES 1 QUART)

- 1 cup hibiscus flowers
- 3 1/2 cups water
- 1 cup dried apricots
- 1 cup dried cranberries
- 1/4 cup sugar
- 5 Tbs. chile sal (p. 161)
- 1/4 cup lemon juice

METHOD

1. Rinse hibiscus flowers to remove any dirt or debris. In a saucepan, cover them with 3 1/2 cups of water and bring to a boil. Lower the heat and simmer for 15 minutes. Allow to cool.
2. In a blender, place the hibiscus tea and flowers and all other ingredients and blend until totally smooth, with no chunks.

Spoon this chamoy on fruit cups, slices of jícama, mango, even cucumbers, or use it as a condiment or a dip with either raw vegetable or corn tortilla chips.

The chamoy can be refrigerated, in an airtight container, for 2 months.

NOPAL PICO DE GALLO

Chef Luna Vela works in Austin, Texas. She was born in Monterrey and at nine years of age moved to the Rio Grande Valley. Moving to Austin for college, she continued her deep-rooted love for the traditions and flavors of the Texas Mexican region. She brings that passion to life in her unique take on the classic pico de gallo, swapping out tomatoes for fresh, tangy nopal. It's a vibrant twist that celebrates the rich culinary heritage of the region—one delicious bite at a time!

INGREDIENTS (MAKES 2 CUPS)

- 2 nopales (cactus paddles), small dice
- 1 Tbs. salt
- 1/2 white onion, small dice
- 2 serrano chiles, finely minced
- 1/2 bunch cilantro, finely chopped
- juice of 1 lime
- salt to taste

METHOD

1. In a bowl, place the diced nopales, sprinkle them with salt, and mix vigorously until they exude the gooey, viscous mucilage. Rinse off the mucilage in cold water and pat dry with paper towels.
2. In a clean bowl, place the rinsed cactus and all the other ingredients, including the lime juice, and stir to combine well. Taste and correct the salt.

Serve as you would traditional pico de gallo. Chef Luna recommends using this as a topping for mesquitamal (p. 30).

CASHEW CRUMBLE

Brazil is the origin of cashews, but today these nuts are universal, enjoyed globally. Along with pepitas, pine nuts, and sesame seeds, they make a delicious layer of flavor to complete a dish. Sprinkle this tart, lemon-flavored cashew crumble over enchiladas or even add it as a crunchy bite to vegetable tacos.

INGREDIENTS (MAKES 1/2 CUP)

- 1 cup raw cashews
- 1/2 tsp. nutritional yeast
- 1/8 tsp. garlic powder
- 1 Tbs. lemon juice
- 1/4 tsp. salt

METHOD

Preheat oven to 350°F

1. Cover the cashews with boiling water and let them sit for 2 hours, then drain.
2. In a spice grinder or small blender, add the cashews and all other ingredients and pulse to combine and make a crumbly, loose paste.
3. Spread the mixture evenly on a small cookie sheet and bake for 5 minutes, just enough time so that the cashews begin to acquire a little color.

Allow the cashew crumble to cool. Store in the refrigerator in an airtight container for up to 7 days.

QUESO DE ALMENDRAS

Nutritional yeast may not be a traditional ingredient in Texas Mexican cooking, but fermentation and yeast have long been part of our culinary heritage. Think of tepache (p. 183), the lightly fizzy drink made from pineapple skins and the yeast that lives there, or pulque and tequila, both born from the natural fermentation of the agave plant. These ancient techniques remind us that yeast has always played a role in Indigenous Mexican kitchens.

Though nutritional yeast gained popularity in the US around the 1960s outside of Latinx communities (Denenberg, 2023), today, more and more Mexican American chefs are embracing this nutritious, umami-rich ingredient in creative new ways. This queso de almendras is a fresh take on tradition—tangy, nutty, and deeply satisfying. It's a new creation, yes, but one that feels right at home in the evolving story of Texas Mexican cuisine. I hope you find it as delicious as I do!

INGREDIENTS (MAKES 1 CUP)

- 1 cup raw almonds
- 4 tsp. lime juice
- 4 tsp. white distilled vinegar
- 4 Tbs. avocado oil
- 4 Tbs. water
- 3 tsp. nutritional yeast
- 1/2 tsp. salt

METHOD

Preheat oven to 350°F

1. In a medium saucepan, bring 3 cups of water to a rolling boil. Add the almonds and blanch for exactly 60 seconds, no more. Drain onto a colander and rinse under cold water to cool the almonds. Remove the skin from the almonds.
2. Place the almonds and all the other ingredients in a small blender or food processor to make a very smooth paste. This will take several minutes, depending on your appliance.
3. Using a spatula or spoon, place the almond paste onto a double cheese cloth. Wrap it and shape into a square or round cake that is 1/2-inch high.
4. Place the wrapped cake on a cookie sheet and bake in a 350°F oven for 15 minutes. Allow to cool completely.

Will keep in the refrigerator for 7 days.

CHILE ANCHO EN ESCABECHE

Bright chile strips get softened while marinating in this combination of both sweet and briny ingredients. I sometimes eat the strips just by themselves.

INGREDIENTS (MAKES 2 CUPS)

- 2 1/2 oz. chiles anchos, deseeded, deveined
- 1/2 cup white onion, small dice
- 1 clove garlic, minced
- 1 sprig fresh or 1/8 tsp. dried thyme
- 1/2 cup distilled white vinegar
- 1/2 cup canola or other flavorless vegetable oil
- 2 tsp. piloncillo or brown sugar
- 2 tsp. salt

METHOD

1. Slice deseeded and deveined chiles into 1/8-inch-thick strips. Set aside.
2. In a small bowl, whisk together the oil, vinegar, piloncillo or sugar, and salt to emulsify.
3. Add the chiles, onion, garlic, and thyme and combine thoroughly.
4. Place in a tightly sealed glass container and refrigerate for at least 8 hours or overnight so that the flavors combine and the chiles soften.

Serve as a topping on tacos or add to salads. This makes a great topping on sautéed Jerusalem artichokes (p. 131) or sautéed chayote (p. 123).

Keeps up to 6 months in the refrigerator.

CHILE SAL

Grinding seeds into powder is an ancient tradition in the Texas Mexican region. Enchanted Rock, Texas, is the site of what are called bedrock mortars, which are large boulders sticking out of the ground with carved-out bowls that were used to grind seeds, nuts, and other ingredients. From El Paso to Victoria to McAllen, ancestors made mortars out of wood and granite and other stones, many dating over thousands of years ago (Potter, 2022). To this day, making powders to enhance culinary enjoyment continues, with this chile sal a prime example.

INGREDIENTS (MAKES 3/4 CUP)

- 1 oz. chiles guajillos (about 5 chiles)
- 1/4 oz. chipotle chile (not in adobo) (about 1 small chile)
- 1/4 oz. pasilla chile (about 1 chile)
- salt in a ratio of 1 to 5

METHOD

1. In a spice grinder, grind all of the chiles into a very fine chile powder.
2. Measure the chile powder in a measuring cup or using a measuring spoon. Add salt to the chile powder in a ratio of 1 part salt to 5 parts chile powder. Mix well.

Sprinkle on fruit of all kinds and on your favorite dish instead of just salt. You can also rim your margarita glass with this delicious chile sal powder.

Store in an airtight container.

CHILE SERRANO VINAIGRETTE

The flavor of chile serrano is herbaceous, so it's a perfect vinaigrette for salad greens. More and more chile vendors are letting go of the notion that heat is the determining factor for choosing chiles. Focusing only on the level of heat loses sight of the many flavors that chiles can offer a dish.

Capsaicin is the chemical in chiles that burns the skin, and it is located mainly in the seeds and inner membranes of the skin. Sometimes it's necessary to remove the capsaicin in order to highlight the flavor and aroma of the chile. That's the case with this dressing, where the seeds and white membrane are removed.

INGREDIENTS (MAKES 3/4 CUP)

- 2 Tbs. deseeded, deveined serrano chile, minced
- 1/4 cup extra virgin olive oil
- 1/4 cup white vinegar
- 1/4 tsp. salt

METHOD

In a mortar and pestle, mash the serrano chile with 1 Tbs. of the olive oil until it forms a smooth paste. Add the remaining ingredients and whisk together to emulsify. Alternately, you can use a shaker bottle and shake until emulsified.

CREMA DE CAJÚ (ANACARDO / NUEZ DE LA INDIA) | CASHEW CREAM

Cashews are native to Brazil but are now enjoyed worldwide, although I can't find one term in Spanish that everyone can agree is a good name. Anacardo, cajú, and nuez de la India are three names that I've found throughout Mexico, and in Texas we just use the English word, cashew. I love this cream because it is a versatile topping for so many of the dishes in this book. After you make this first batch, you can adjust the amount of water in subsequent batches to make a thicker or thinner cream. Try the taste and then explore how many ways you can use this creamy condiment.

INGREDIENTS (MAKES 2 CUPS)

- 1 cup raw cashews, soaked in water at least 2 hours and preferably overnight
- 3/4 cup water
- 1 1/2 Tbs. fresh lemon juice
- 1/2 tsp. salt

METHOD

Place all ingredients in a blender, including the water, and blend until completely smooth and creamy. This will take from 1 to 3 minutes, depending on your blender.

JÍCAMA CRANBERRY CONSERVE

Thanksgiving dinner at our family always included two memorable condiments that are Native American: serrano chile salsa and cranberry sauce. I've included a serrano salsa on p. 169, and here is a zesty recipe for cranberry sauce that takes a twist, with tangerine, ginger, and sultanas.

INGREDIENTS (MAKES 3 CUPS)

- 3/4 lb. fresh cranberries
- 1/2 cup jícama, small dice
- 1 tsp. grated peeled ginger
- 1/2 cup sultanas (golden raisins)
- 1/3 cup freshly squeezed tangerine juice
- 4-inch x 1-inch tangerine peel, pith removed
- 2/3 cup light brown sugar
- 2 Tbs. sugar (optional)

METHOD

1. Place all the ingredients in a saucepan and bring to a boil, stirring to dissolve the sugars.
2. Lower the heat and simmer, uncovered, for about 15 minutes until the cranberries begin to pop open.
3. Remove from heat and let cool.

You can serve the conserve immediately or store it in the refrigerator for up to 2 days. To me it tastes better after about 12 hours in the fridge.

MOJO DE AJO

Camarón al mojo de ajo (shrimp in garlic sauce) is typically known for featuring the famous oil and garlic sauce, but this mojo is a versatile condiment for just about any dish. Mojo de ajo is actually a paste, and it is traditional also in Cuba and the Caribbean. It's great with yucca root, and you will find delicious ways to include it on tacos and other dishes. It's culinary gold.

INGREDIENTS (MAKES 4 CUPS)

- 2 cups extra virgin olive oil
- 1 1/2 cups peeled garlic cloves
- 1/2 cup fresh lime juice
- 1/2 tsp. salt, or to taste

METHOD

Preheat oven to 325F

1. Combine the garlic, oil, and salt in a baking pan and bake for 45 minutes.
2. Remove from the oven and add the lime juice. Return to the oven and bake an additional 20 minutes.
3. Mash the garlic mixture into a coarse paste using either a large spoon or a potato masher.

Store the mojo de ajo in a jar in the refrigerator for up to 3 months.

CHILE PIQUÍN SALSA

This tiny chile was a constant in my family's backyard in San Antonio, growing lush and rampant. Sometimes the plants would die out, but they'd always eventually return. It's just part of our environment in this region of the world that is South Texas and Northeastern Mexico. This salsa has an interesting balance as I combine sharp tomatillos with roasted tomatoes.

INGREDIENTS (MAKES 2 CUPS)

- 6 piquín chiles
- 3 Roma tomatoes
- 1/2 lb. tomatillos
- 1/4 cup cilantro, chopped
- 1 tsp. salt

METHOD

1. On a comal (griddle) or cast iron skillet, roast the Roma tomatoes until they are partially cooked with dark spots. Set aside.
2. In a saucepan, cover the tomatillos with water and bring to a boil. Simmer until the color changes and they are cooked. Drain.
3. In a blender, place the tomatillos, tomatoes, chiles, cilantro, and salt. Blend until smooth

Serve warm or at room temperature.

SERRANO CRUDO SALSA

Serrano chiles are my favorite flavor because they have an herbal taste that adds freshness to every bite. I remove all the seeds and membranes in the chiles to reduce the heat and increase the flavor. It's still a very hot salsa but is bursting with beautiful flavor and has a creamy texture.

This salsa is pure serrano flavor with no other ingredient: no onion, no garlic, no nothing. I hope you will fall in love with the flavor, as I surely have.

INGREDIENTS (MAKES ONE PINT)

- 8 oz. fresh chile serrano, deseeded, deveined
- 4 fl. oz. water
- 4 fl. oz. canola oil
- 1/2 tsp. salt

METHOD

1. Cut off the stems from the chiles serranos and slice in half lengthwise.
2. Using a small spoon, carve out the white vein and scoop out all of the seeds.
3. Place the deseeded, deveined chiles in a blender with the water, oil, and salt and blend until smooth and creamy. Adjust the salt.

Serve immediately or hold in the refrigerator for about 2 days to preserve the green, herbal flavor. Re-emulsify as needed.

BROWN VEGETABLE STOCK

The cooking in our home added mainly plain water to dishes, like enchilada sauces and soups, as do most of the recipes in this book. But for those times when the dish needs a heartier, more robust base, use this brown stock. It will intensify the flavor of the recipe and deepen the color.

INGREDIENTS (MAKES 1 GALLON)

- 1 gallon plus 16 oz. cold water
- 1 1/2 lbs. onion, skin on, quartered
- 3/4 lb. carrots, sliced crosswise into 2-inch pieces
- 3/4 lb. celery, sliced crosswise into 2-inch pieces
- 1 lb. zucchini, sliced crosswise into 2-inch pieces
- 1 lb. mushrooms, washed and coarsely chopped
- 1 lb. ripe tomatoes, quartered
- 1 garlic head, unpeeled
- 2 Tbs. extra virgin olive oil
- 1/4 laurel leaf
- 1/2 tsp. crushed black peppercorns
- 1/4 tsp. dried thyme
- 4 parsley stems

METHOD

1. In a large stock pot, over high heat, heat the olive oil and cook the onions, carrots, and celery until they acquire dark spots, about 5 minutes.
2. Add the tomatoes, zucchini, garlic, and mushrooms and cook for another 5 minutes, stirring as needed.
3. Add 1 gallon and 16 oz. cold water to the vegetables, along with the 1/4 laurel leaf, black peppercorns, thyme, and parsley. Bring to a slow simmer, lower the heat, and simmer for 45 minutes. Strain through a fine mesh sieve.

I use this stock in chile poblano rice (p. 143).

The stock can be frozen for later use, up to 3 months. It will keep in the refrigerator for 1 week.

WHITE VEGETABLE STOCK

For many of the recipes in this book, water is called for, but when you want a more intense flavor, use this stock. Different from the brown vegetable stock (p. 171), this is for dishes where you need the color to remain bright and white and the flavor to be mild and delicate. The stock also has the slightest tinge of sweetness.

INGREDIENTS (MAKES 1 GALLON)

- 1 gallon plus 16 oz. cold water
- 3 lbs. onion, peeled, cut into quarters
- 1 1/2 lbs. parsnips, washed, peeled, and cut into 2-inch lengths
- 1 1/2 lbs. celery, washed
- 2 garlic heads, unpeeled, cloves loosened
- 4 oz. white button mushrooms, washed, coarsely chopped
- 1 Tbs. olive oil
- 1/4 tsp. crushed black pepper
- 1/4 laurel leaf
- 1 sprig fresh or 1/4 tsp. dried thyme
- sprig of parsley

METHOD

1. Heat the oil on medium heat in a large stock pot or Dutch oven. Add all the vegetables, cover, and decrease the heat to low. Cook for 12 minutes so that the vegetables begin to soften and release juices.
2. Add 1 gallon plus 16 oz. cold water. Add the black pepper, laurel leaf, thyme, and parsley. Simmer, uncovered, for 45 minutes. Skim off the scum with a large spoon. Strain through a fine mesh sieve.

The stock will keep in the refrigerator for up to 7 days. It can also be frozen for up to 3 months.

CHAPTER 8

BEVERAGES

GOLDEN APPLES
SM NAVEL ORANGES
SM GALA APPLES
ROMA TOMATOES

BAJICOPO

Bajicopo is an agua fresca that is both refreshing and rich tasting. It is similar to horchata but is made with whole grain wheat (wheat berries) instead of rice. In this recipe I avoid the need to cook the whole grain wheat by using bulgur wheat, which is the wheat berry that has been cracked and already cooked. This makes the agua fresca process speedier.

Wheat arrived in the Texas Mexican region in the1600s, when Spanish expeditions began to reach this northern region. In 1689 and 1690, Alonso de León led two expeditions to the area near Eagle Pass, Texas, and arrived with foods that were staples of the Spanish diet like beef, wine, and, of course, wheat (Montaño, 2023). This delicious beverage is an example of how newly arrived European products were interpreted through Native techniques and an Indigenous palate.

INGREDIENTS (MAKES 2 QUARTS)

- 1/2 lb. bulgur wheat (optional: soak the bulgur wheat in water for at least 30 minutes before blending for a smoother texture)
- 1/4 cup sugar
- 1/4 cup water
- 2-inch stick of canela (Mexican cinnamon)
- 4 clove buds
- 2 quarts water
- simple syrup

FOR THE SIMPLE SYRUP

- 3/4 cup sugar
- 3/4 cup water

METHOD

1. To make the simple syrup, heat the water and sugar until the sugar is completely dissolved. Let it cool completely.
2. In a blender, place all the ingredients, except the simple syrup, and blend on high until smooth. Strain through a fine mesh sieve. Add the simple syrup to sweeten, a little at a time, according to your taste.

Keep cold and serve over ice.

CRANBERRY ROSEMARY CHAMPAGNE COCKTAIL

Cranberries are a Native American fruit, deeply embedded in the cultural and culinary traditions of Indigenous peoples. This cocktail pairs the tart, vibrant flavor of cranberries with the woodsy, aromatic essence of rosemary, creating a drink that is both refreshing and steeped in history. Archaeological sites in the Northeastern United States, dating as far back as 1000 BC to AD 95, reveal evidence of ancient bogs of cranberries (*Vaccinium macrocarpon*) and their widespread use by Native peoples. In Spanish, cranberries are called arándano rojo, but their original name among the Lenni Lenape people was ibimi, which translates to "bitter" or "sour berries."

The Lenni Lenape, also known as the Delaware, were among the original inhabitants of the Northeastern United States who harvested cranberries. Over time, they were tragically forced from their homelands, first to Ohio and later even farther west. By 1859, many had sought refuge in Texas as they fled continued displacement. However, even in Texas, their struggle persisted, and by 1872, most had been relocated again, this time to Oklahoma. Despite these injustices, the Lenni Lenape preserved their rich traditions, including the use of cranberries for medicine, cooking, and dyeing textiles ("Delaware Indians," n.d.).

Texas, often overlooked in this history, played an important role as a place of both refuge and struggle for the Lenni Lenape. By including them in this cookbook, we honor their legacy. This cranberry rosemary champagne cocktail, perfect for winter holidays, is a delicious way to celebrate that legacy. The stories they carry connect us to a shared past and a hopeful future.

INGREDIENTS (MAKES 12 COCKTAILS)

- 12 oz. fresh cranberries
- 1/2 cup fresh rosemary (remove the leaves, or needles, from the sprig)
- 1 cup water
- 12 oz. (1 1/2 cups) vodka
- 3 bottles sparkling sweet rosé (750 ml each) like a sparkling Moscato
- 12 sprigs of fresh rosemary for garnish

METHOD

1. Place cranberries, rosemary needles, and water in a saucepan and bring to a boil. Lower the heat and simmer, covered, for 45 minutes.
2. Strain through a fine mesh sieve, pressing the mixture to strain out the flesh of the cooked cranberries, leaving the skins behind. The mixture will have the consistency of a purée.
3. After the cranberry-rosemary purée has cooled, add the vodka and chill in the refrigerator. The pectin in the cranberries will cause it to gel, so use a whisk to liquefy the mixture back into a runny purée.

To assemble the cocktail, fill a double old-fashioned glass with ice and pour in 1 oz. of the vodka cranberry purée. Fill with the sparkling Moscato and stir gently. Add a sprig of rosemary for garnish.

MESQUITE AGUA FRESCA

Mesquite is our precious, although long-ago forgotten, culinary heritage. For millennia, before the arrival of corn from down south, it was mesquite that was central to our survival and to our culture. Even after corn arrived in Texas and Northeastern Mexico around 700 CE, mesquite continued to be the only dependable source of nutrition and culinary enjoyment. In fact, mesquite is so central to our history and survival that we have been called "la gente del mezquite" (people of the mesquite) (Valdés, 1995).

This recipe recalls how ancestors, to make this beverage, would crush mesquite pods in wooden mortars, sometimes directly in holes in the earth for added flavor (Cabeza de Vaca, 1542).

INGREDIENTS (MAKES 4 CUPS)

- 5 oz. mesquite pods, frozen
- 8 cups water
- 1–2 Tbs. maple syrup

METHOD

1. You may want to freeze the mesquite pods, depending on where you picked or obtained them. Freezing kills little gray bugs (weevils or bruchid beetles) that may have gotten into the pods. If there are little holes in the pods, those are exit holes where the bruchids dug their way out. The bruchids are harmless, though, so it isn't necessary to freeze the pods. Make sure to thaw the pods completely before proceeding to make the agua fresca.
2. In a large saucepan, heat 8 cups of water until it begins to boil. Add the mesquite beans and boil them until they become soft. This may take up to 45 minutes, depending on how dry the pods are. Up to one-half of the water will evaporate. Allow the pods and water to cool.
3. In a blender, place the cooled mesquite pods along with the water. Add additional water to make 4 cups. Pulse the blender for just a few seconds to slightly crush the pods, breaking them apart to release their sweet juice. The seeds are very hard, so they will remain intact.
4. Strain the crushed mesquite solution through a fine mesh sieve, pressing on the pods to extract as much juice as possible. Discard the pods.
5. Add the maple syrup according to your taste, stirring to dissolve completely. Refrigerate the agua fresca for an hour or longer.

Serve the mesquite agua fresca over ice.

Mesquite pods, purchased online (photo by author)

Tepache in a Mexican vitrolero (photo by author)

TEPACHE

Tepache is made from pineapple peel. The delicious pineapple is from a river landscape that covers three countries: present-day Brazil, Paraguay, and Argentina. A cultural and economically important food, the pineapple was used medicinally and made into alcohol, and its fibers were woven into clothes and robes and also used for bow strings. By the time of the conquest, the pineapple had travelled north to Mexico and into the Caribbean where Christopher Columbus encountered it on the Guadeloupe islands in November 1493 ("The Prickly Meanings of the Pineapple," 2021).

When the pineapple traveled north to Mexico, locals fermented and sweetened the pineapple peel to create this pre-Conquest drink, tepache. For fermentation, I use a large Mexican glass barrel (vitrolero), that is commonly used for aguas frescas. The drink looks amazing and tastes refreshing.

INGREDIENTS (MAKES 2 QUARTS)

- 1 ripe pineapple
- 1 piloncillo cone
- 3 clove buds
- 3 allspice berries
- 2 2-inch sticks of canela (Mexican cinnamon)
- 2 oranges (1 1/4 cups)
- 2 quarts water
- 1 orange, sliced, for garnish
- 1 lime, sliced, for garnish

METHOD

1. Rinse the pineapple very gently so as not to remove the yeast that lives on the surface. Slice off all the peel.
2. In a large glass container, preferably a Mexican vitrolero made for agua fresca, place all of the peel. Mash the cloves and allspice in a mortar and add them, along with the orange juice, piloncillo, and cinnamon, to 2 quarts of water. Mix well and cover with a cloth, tied to the opening with a string. Place the container in a location away from direct light and allow it to ferment at room temperature for 3–5 days. The piloncillo cone will dissolve as you stir the tepache daily.
3. As it ferments, bubbles will form on the surface. Taste the tepache after 3 days and if the flavor is just right, slightly bubbly, then it's ready. Depending on how warm the room is, fermentation may be sooner or later, but 3–5 days makes a good tepache. Chill the tepache.

Serve the tepache very cold and garnish with slices of orange and lime.

YAUPON HOLLY TEA

I made this tea recipe with the leaves of the yaupon holly tree that grows in my front window. Yaupon holly was enjoyed by ancestors for its naturally occurring caffeine. The tea was brewed for medicinal purposes, since it is loaded with antioxidants (Yaupon Tea, 2021).

Unfortunately, some misguided history states that this drink causes one to vomit, hence the scientific name, *Ilex vomitoria*. But the evidence indicates that it happened only when the drink was willingly imbibed in excess for that purpose, much like drinking a gallon of coffee at one gulp (Tejas > Caddo Fundamentals > Mississippian World, n.d.)

Because of its coffee-like color, it was sometimes called the black drink, and along the Gulf Coast it was drunk using beautiful shell cups made from the large mollusk, the lightning whelk, caught in the Gulf of Mexico (Driess, 2022). I love the invigorating taste of this lightly caffeinated drink.

INGREDIENTS (MAKES 1 CUP DRIED TEA LEAVES)

- 2 cups fresh yaupon holly leaves
- Water as needed
- Sweetening options including honey, maple syrup, or raw agave nectar

METHOD

Preheat oven to 300°F

TO PREPARE THE TEA LEAVES

1. Wash the yaupon holly leaves and then dry them with a salad spinner.
2. Place the dry leaves on a large cookie sheet or sheet pan and place in a 300°F oven for 10 minutes. The leaves will become dry and brittle. Make sure not to burn them. Remove them and let them cool. Crush them coarsely and save in an airtight container.

TO MAKE THE TEA

Place 1 Tbs. dried yaupon holly leaves in hot water (190°F) and let steep for 5–8 minutes. You may sweeten according to your taste with honey, maple syrup, or raw agave nectar

Serve hot or ice cold.

CHAPTER 9

SWEETS

AVOCADO POPSICLE | PALETA DE AGUACATE

The creaminess in this popsicle comes from the lush avocado which takes so well to sweetening. The surprising addition of tomatillo adds a delicious combination of tartness and umami. It's perfect for your next brunch party dessert.

INGREDIENTS (MAKES 6 POPSICLES)

- 6 oz. avocado
- 3 oz. tomatillo, quartered
- 6 Tbs. fresh lime juice
- 12 Tbs. (3/4 cup) simple syrup

FOR THE SIMPLE SYRUP

- 3/4 cup sugar
- 3/4 cup water

METHOD

1. To make the simple syrup, heat the water and sugar until the sugar is completely dissolved. Let it cool completely.
2. Place all the ingredients in a blender and blend until smooth. Taste the sweetness and add more simple syrup as necessary, 1 Tbs. at a time.
3. Fill popsicle molds (3 oz. size) and freeze for 4 hours or until frozen solid.

ATOLE DE MESQUITE | MESQUITE PORRIDGE

Atole is at the heart of traditional Mexican cooking, and in the South Texas and Northeastern Mexico region, it is made most often today with corn flour. But long before corn arrived, the main ingredient for atole was mesquite, and I think it's time that we reclaimed this historically important and nutritious food. Mesquite contains twice the amount of protein as corn and three times the amount of dietary fiber (FoodData Central, n.d.).

Coahuiltecans would prepare a type of porridge by digging a hole in the earth where they would place mesquite pods, then fill with water. They'd pound the pods using a thick wooden stump to create a porridge that was sweetened with some of the earth (Cabeza de Vaca, 1542). Of course, the earth was not polluted as it is in many places these days.

For this recipe I combine the mesquite flour with corn and honor both traditions.

INGREDIENTS (SERVES 8)

- 5 oz. mesquite pods
- 6–8 cups water
- 1/2 cup masa harina (corn flour)
- 1 3–4-inch stick canela (Mexican cinnamon)
- 2 Tbs. piloncillo

METHOD

1. You may want to freeze the mesquite pods, depending on where you picked or obtained them. Freezing kills little gray bugs (weevils or bruchid beetles) that may have gotten into the pods. If there are little holes in the pods, those are exit holes where the bruchids dug their way out. The bruchids are harmless, though, so it isn't necessary to freeze the pods. If you choose to freeze them, make sure to thaw the pods completely.
2. In a large saucepan, heat 6–8 cups of water until it begins to boil. Add the mesquite beans and boil them until they become soft. This may take up to 45 minutes, depending on how dry the pods are. Up to one-half of the water will evaporate. If necessary, add clean water to make 4 cups. Allow the pods and water to cool.
3. In a blender, place the cooled mesquite pods, along with 2 cups of the mesquite liquid. Pulse the blender for just a few seconds to slightly crush the pods, breaking them apart to release their sweet juice. The seeds are very hard, so they will remain intact.
4. Strain the crushed mesquite juice through a fine mesh sieve, pressing on the pods to extract as much juice as possible. Discard the pods and set the liquid aside. You will have about 2 1/2 cups.
5. In a saucepan, heat the remaining 2 cups of water in which you boiled the mesquite pods. Add 1/2 cup corn flour and whisk thoroughly. Add the mesquite juice, canela, and piloncillo. Cook on a slow simmer until the atole thickens, about 10 minutes.

Serve hot.

Nicuatole (photo by author)

NICUATOLE

Gelatinization of the starch molecules in corn is one of the culinary discoveries of Mesoamerica. When heated with water, the corn starch granules begin to break down, and at about 140°F gelatin begins to form. This important discovery is used by cooks worldwide, including in many Chinese dishes that use corn starch as a thickener.

This gelatin dessert recipe is made with corn flour (masa harina). It's an example of a dish with ancient roots but with total delicious currency today (Luis et al., 2023). Nicuatole has travelled northward from its origins in the Oaxaca region, and I like to make it for dessert or anytime as a nutritious, delicious gelatin treat.

The decorative pink color is traditionally made with ground dried cochineal beetles that live on cactus paddles, but that's hard to find, so I use regular red food coloring in this recipe.

INGREDIENTS (MAKES ONE DOZEN)

- 1 1/2 cups masa harina (corn flour)
- 5-inch stick canela (Mexican cinnamon)
- 1/3 cup sugar
- 4 cups water

FOR THE RED SUGAR

- 1/4 cup granulated sugar
- 6 drops red food coloring

METHOD

TO MAKE THE RED SUGAR

In a deep bowl, add granulated sugar and red food coloring. Whisk the sugar to combine with the coloring until the sugar is uniformly red. Add more drops of coloring as needed.

TO MAKE THE NICUATOLE

1. In a heavy bottom saucepan, add the masa harina, sugar, and water and stir to combine so there are no lumps. Add the cinnamon stick and bring to a low simmer.
2. Cook on low for 30 minutes, stirring continuously, making sure it does not stick to the bottom. The mixture will become very thick, so keep scraping the bottom and stirring.
3. Distribute the nicuatole among 6 six-oz. muffin tins or other decorative containers.
4. Sprinkle a layer of red sugar on top of each filled muffin tin and then allow to cool.

Unmold onto plates and serve at room temperature with slices of fruit like papaya or dragon fruit.

PECAN BLUEBERRY CHIA PUDDING

I include this recipe to highlight the amazing reflowering and resurgence of the tiny chia seed not just in Texas and Northeastern Mexico but all over the world.

Native to Mexico and Guatemala, chia was one of the important food staples that nourished the peoples of Mesoamerica for 4,500 years, along with corn and beans. But over generations it fell into disuse until it was almost completely forgotten. There are two reasons for this. First, the lands used to grow chia for millennia were taken over by new crops and animals from Europe. Second, Spanish conquest killed over 95 percent of the Mexican population, with a decline from 22 million Indigenous people in 1529 to only 1 million in 1620 (Anacleto et al., 2018). This figure is always heartbreaking to report and write.

It was around 1990 that in three Mexican states, Puebla, Guerrero, and Jalisco, a small group of farmers began to plant chia crops, in traditional ways, and their efforts succeeded wildly. Today over thirty countries cultivate it. The chia seeds market is projected to grow from $1.39 billion in 2024 to $7.38 billion in 2033 (Markets, 2025). There is hope that if we support local family farmers who grow chia, we will increasingly benefit from the nutritional properties of this Mexican ancestral crop.

INGREDIENTS (SERVES 4)

- 1/2 cup pecans
- 3 cups water
- 9 Tbs. chia seeds
- 4–6 Tbs. maple syrup according to taste
- 1/2 cup blueberries, coarsely chopped
- 12 blueberries for garnish

METHOD

1. In a blender, place the pecans and water and blend on high until completely smooth and milky.
2. In a large bowl, add the pecan liquid and 4 Tbs. maple syrup. Stir well and taste the level of sweetness, adding more maple syrup as needed. Sprinkle in the chia seeds and stir to combine thoroughly. Let the mixture sit for 10 minutes.
3. Add the chopped blueberries and stir to combine.
4. Refrigerate for at least 2 hours or overnight so that the mixture thickens completely.

Serve garnished with 3 whole blueberries on top.

Quinoa pancakes (photo by author)

QUINOA PANCAKES

Quinoa is a seed from a tall leafy plant originating in the area surrounding Lake Titicaca, in Bolivia and Peru. It is now popular worldwide, and I like to include it in many dishes, including panqueques (pancakes). Although far off in the Andes, quinoa is like many of our indigenous plants (amaranth, yaupon holly, etc.) in that it offers a look at the richness that our past traditions offer for today. The United Nations General Assembly declared 2013 the "International Year of Quinoa." The goal was to let more people know about the importance of indigenous ancestral customs and the power they have for healing poverty and for teaching us how to live without destroying nature. Sustainable dining is also delicious.

I use bourbon vanilla in this recipe because it gives the quinoa pancakes a pleasant underlying tang, but you can use regular vanilla and they'll taste delicious. You can use whole wheat or regular all-purpose flour.

INGREDIENTS (MAKES 8 PANCAKES)

- 1 1/2 cups whole wheat flour or all-purpose flour
- 1 Tbs. baking powder
- 1 tsp. baking soda
- 1 tsp. salt
- 2 Tbs. sugar
- 1 1/4 cups soy milk (unsweetened)
- 1/2 cup water
- 1/2 tsp. bourbon vanilla extract or plain vanilla extract
- 2 tsp. apple cider vinegar
- 2 Tbs. canola oil
- 1 cup cooked quinoa (allow it to cool before adding)
- additional canola oil to coat the griddle

METHOD

1. Sift together all the dry ingredients and place in a large mixing bowl.
2. Make a hole in the middle of the dry ingredients and pour in the liquid ingredients: soy milk, water, bourbon vanilla extract, vinegar, and canola oil. Using a spatula, mix all the ingredients together to make a batter that is still a bit lumpy, then add the cooled quinoa, mixing it well. **IMPORTANT:** Let the batter rest for 10–15 minutes.
3. Heat a griddle on medium to low heat, between 300°F and 350°F. Apply a thin layer of oil to the griddle and pour about 1/3 cup of batter for each pancake. Cook for about 3 minutes until bubbles form and the edges look partially cooked, then flip the pancake, applying more oil if needed. Cook the other side for another 2 or 3 minutes.

Serve immediately, garnished with blueberries or other fruit, and maple or other syrup. Note that maple syrup is indigenous to Mexico and the US, a food from pre-European contact.

Praying at the Tamōx Talōm Food Forest Project in San Antonio, led by the Tap Pilam Coahuiltecan Nation, a tribal community that celebrates their lineage back to the Coahuiltecan people.

CONCLUSION

A PARTNERSHIP WITH THE PLANT COMMUNITY

As I bring *The Texas Mexican Plant-Based Cookbook* to a close, I want to reflect on the ideas that connect the recipes and histories in these pages to a broader vision of the future. This book is more than a celebration of the past; it is also a blueprint for a sustainable and respectful relationship with the natural world, rooted in the philosophy of partnership with the plant community, a partnership that can restore our health. The setting of many of the photographs you see here is the Tamōx Talōm Food Forest Project in San Antonio, led by the Tap Pilam Coahuiltecan Nation, a tribal community composed of individuals who proudly trace their lineage back to the Coahuiltecan people. It is an inspiring example of what the future can hold when we reimagine our relationship with the land.

The Tamōx Talōm Food Forest is not merely a place where food is grown; it is a living demonstration of the way we used to live and represents an alternative approach to agriculture and community. Unlike conventional farming, which often prioritizes yield and efficiency above all else, a food forest is guided by the principle of mutual respect between humans and the natural world. It operates not as a managed commodity-driven system but as an ecosystem where plants, animals, and humans coexist in harmony. This philosophy is evident in every aspect of the food forest, from the way plants are arranged to foster biodiversity to the minimal intervention by humans in the natural processes of growth and regeneration.

The stark difference between a food forest and agribusiness cannot be overstated. Agribusiness relies on monocultures and control, treating plants as commodities to be harvested and sold. Rows of crops stand in isolation, requiring heavy inputs of fertilizer, pesticides, and irrigation to sustain them. In contrast, a food forest mimics the complexity and resilience of a natural forest, where diverse species support one another. The pictures you can see are not of tidy rows but of lush, interwoven vegetation that grows in partnership with its environment. Here, plants flourish not as isolated units but as members of a larger community, each contributing to and benefiting from the whole.

This shift in philosophy—from control to partnership—is profound and urgently needed. As we face the dual crises of environmental degradation and food insecurity, projects like the Tamōx Talōm Food Forest point the way toward a more sustainable and equitable future. By embracing the principles of food forests, we can create systems that provide nourishment while regenerating the land, fostering biodiversity, and strengthening the bond between humans and the earth.

The recipes in this book, rooted in the traditions of Texas Mexican cuisine, reflect this philosophy of interconnectedness. They showcase how delicious and nourishing meals can be, created with ingredients that are part of a larger story—one of resilience, creativity, and harmony with the land. Cooking these dishes is an act of celebration and awareness, a way to honor the bond we share with the plants that sustain us. It is a road to health, for ourselves and for our planet.

Through these recipes, we are invited to see food not just as a product but as a connection. The histories behind each dish—the cultivation of corn through nixtamalization, the foraging of wild greens, the roasting of chiles—speak to the deep knowledge and respect that Indigenous Mexican American communities have cultivated for generations. These practices remind us that cooking is not merely a task; it is an opportunity to engage with the earth and with one another.

As you explore the recipes and stories in this book, I hope they inspire you to think about food in new ways. Consider not only the flavors and techniques but also the relationships that make each dish possible: the relationships between plants and soil, between farmers and ecosystems, between cooks and communities. This growing awareness is the first step toward building a more sustainable and equitable food system, one that honors the wisdom of the past while embracing the possibilities of a healthier future.

There are many other projects like the Tamōx Talōm Food Forest, all of them powerful examples of what this future can look like. They remind us that the choices we make about food—how we grow it, prepare it, and share it—are choices about the kind of world we want to live in. By adopting the principles of partnership and respect that guide the food forest, we can create a future that is not only sustainable but also deeply nourishing for both people and the planet.

I invite you to carry the spirit of the food forest into your own kitchens and communities. Cook with intention, celebrate the diversity of plant life, and nurture the connections that sustain us all. Together, we can create a brighter future—one meal, one garden, one food forest at a time.

Thank you for joining me on this journey. May the recipes and philosophies in *The Texas Mexican Plant-Based Cookbook* enrich your table and inspire your vision for a more connected and harmonious world.

With gratitude,
Adán Medrano

LIST OF RECIPES

Acorn Squash with Mole, 46
Ajoblanco, 67
Atole de Mesquite, 190
Avocado and Kidney Bean Salad, 85
Avocado Popsicle, 189
Bajicopo, 177
Bell Pepper Salsa, 152
Botana de Xoconostles, 91
Brown Vegetable Stock, 171
Butter Beans with Poblano Rajas, 109
Cabbage and Potato Gorditas, 52
Cactus and Bean Salad, 86
Calabacita Salteada, 119
Calabacitas con Achiote, 120
Cashew Cream, 164
Cashew Crumble, 158
Cauliflower Filets with Parsley Salsa, 55
Cebollas Encurtidas, 153
Chamoy Casero, 155
Chile Ancho en Escabeche, 160
Chile con Jackfruit, 40
Chile Dulce, 152
Chile Piquín Salsa, 168
Chile Poblano Rice, 143
Chile Sal, 161
Chile Serrano Vinaigrette, 163
Chiles Toreados, 124
Chilled Garlic Soup, 67
Colache de Calabacitas, 127
Cold Mango Soup, 68
Conchitas, 144
Cranberry Rosemary Champagne Cocktail, 178
Crema de Cajú, 164
Enchiladas Mineras, 14
Enchiladas Potosinas, 16
Enfrijoladas, 23
Ensalada de Aguacate con Frijol, 85
Ensalada de Calabacita, 92
Ensalada de Calabacita y Ejote, 95
Ensalada de Garbanzos y Calabacitas, 96
Ensalada de Nopalitos con Frijoles, 86
Entomatadas, 24
Flor de Jamaica en Chile Colorado, 128
Garbanzo and Calabacita Soup with Chipotle, 71
Garbanzo, Mushroom, and Red Chile Dip, 110
Green Corn Soup, 72
Herbed Corn and Jerusalem Artichoke Tart, 56
Hibiscus Flower Drowned Torta, 58
Jícama Cranberry Conserve, 166
Kale and Red Jalapeño Salad, 101
King Trumpet Mushroom and Calabacita Green Enchiladas, 20
Leeks in Tomatillo Salsa, 98
Lentejas Guisadas, 113
Lentejas y Acelga, 114
Lentils with Swiss Chard, 114
Mashed Turnip with Poblano Rajas, 138
Memelas Oaxaqueñas, 62
Mesquitamal, 30
Mesquite Agua Fresca, 180
Mesquite Porridge, 190
Milanesa de Zucchini con Salsa de Rábano, 60
Mojo de Ajo, 167
Mole de Nuez y Mezquite, 48
Mushroom and Green Olive Rice, 147
Mushroom Paella, 148
Mushroom Tacos, 36
Mushroom Tamales, 26
Mushrooms with Calabacita and Corn, 132
Nicuatole, 193

Nopalitos Asados con Vinagreta al Guajillo, 88
Nopalitos with Red Chile, 134
Nopal Pico de Gallo, 156
Paleta de Aguacate, 189
Pecan and Mezquite Mole, 48
Pecan Blueberry Chia Pudding, 194
Pickled Watermelon Rind and Bean Salad, 102
Pipián Ranchero with Jerusalem Artichokes (Sunchokes), 42
Pipián Verde with Yucca and Calabacitas, 44
Posole Rojo, 74
Posole Verde with Mushrooms, 76
Queso de Almendras, 159
Quinoa Pancakes, 197
Sautéed Chayote, 123
Sautéed Jerusalem Artichokes, 131
Serrano Crudo Salsa, 169
Shell Pasta, 144
Sopa de Calabacitas, 78
Sopa de Elote, 81
Sopa Tarasca, 82
Spinach Enchiladas, 18
Tacos de Hongos, 36
Tamales de Habas y Rajas de Chiles Poblanos, 28
Tamales de Hongos, 26
Tepache, 183
Toksel, 115
Tortitas de Papa with Salsa and Salad, 38
Tostadas, 32
Tostadas de Berenjena, 35
Tupinambo Salteado, 131
Turnip and Amaranth in Tomatillo Sauce, 136
Watermelon and Jícama Salad with Cilantro Dressing, 105
White Vegetable Stock, 172
Yaupon Holly Tea, 184
Zucchini Cutlets with Radish Salsa, 60

REFERENCES

Ajmera, Rachael. "7 Surprising Health Benefits of Eggplants." Healthline, June 30, 2017. https://www.healthline.com/nutrition/eggplant-benefits.

Alemán, J. O., J. P. Almandoz, J. P. Frias, and R. J. Galindo. "Obesity among Latinx People in the United States: A Review." *Obesity* 31, no. 2 (2023): 329–37. https://doi.org/10.1002/oby.23638

Anacleto, S., G. Ruiz-Ibarra, R. René, R.-R. de la Torre, R. Reyna, and A. López. "The Chia (*Salvia Hispanica*): Past, Present and Future of an Ancient Mexican Crop." *Australian Journal of Crop Science* 12 (2018): 1626–32. https://doi.org/10.21475/ajcs.18.12.10.p1202.

Apache, Crisosto. "Lozen and Dahteste." *Sovereign Writes* (blog), March 21, 2017. https://crisostoapache.com/lozen-and-dahteste/.

Arreola, D. D. *Tejano South Texas: A Mexican American Cultural Province*. Austin: University of Texas Press, 2002.

Brenner, L. "The Unpleasant Truth about Tex-Mex" [Substack newsletter]. *Brenner Report*, August 5, 2020. https://brennerreport.substack.com/p/the-unpleasant-truth-about-tex-mex.

Bureau, U. C. "Half of People of Dominican and Salvadoran Origin Experienced Material Hardship in 2020." Census.Gov, September 28, 2022. https://www.census.gov/library/stories/2022/09/hardships-wealth-disparities-across-hispanic-groups.html.

Cabeza de Vaca, A. *The Narrative of Cabeza de Vaca*. Lincoln: University of Nebraska Press, 2003[1542].

Carroll, Rachel. "Two Spirit People: How Native and Queer Identities Intersect." *Law Journal for Social Justice*, November 20, 2022. https://lawjournalforsocialjustice.com/2022/11/20/two-spirit-people-how-native-and-queer-identities-intersect/.

Castellanos-Morales, G., K. Y. Ruiz-Mondragón, H. S. Hernández-Rosales, G. Sánchez-de la Vega, N. Gámez, E. Aguirre-Planter, S. Montes-Hernández, R. Lira-Saade, and L. E. Eguiarte. "Tracing Back the Origin of Pumpkins (*Cucurbita pepo ssp. Pepo L.*) in Mexico." *Proceedings of the Royal Society B: Biological Sciences* 286, no. 1908 (2019): 20191440. https://doi.org/10.1098/rspb.2019.1440.

CDC. "How Overweight and Obesity Impacts Your Health." Healthy Weight and Growth, April 25, 2024. https://www.cdc.gov/healthy-weight-growth/food-activity/overweight-obesity-impacts-health.html.

Da-Costa-Rocha, I., B. Bonnlaender, H. Sievers, I. Pischel, and M. Heinrich. "*Hibiscus sabdariffa L.*– A Phytochemical and Pharmacological Review." *Food Chemistry* 165 (2014): 424–43. https://doi.org/10.1016/j.foodchem.2014.05.002.

"Delaware Indians." Texas State Historical Association. Accessed January 11, 2025. https://www.tshaonline.org/handbook/entries/delaware-indians.

Denenberg, Zoe. "What's So 'Nutritional' About Nutritional Yeast?" Epicurious, July 24, 2023. https://www.epicurious.com/ingredients/what-is-nutritional-yeast.

Driess, M. L "Shell Tools." Texas Beyond History, November 2022. https://www.texasbeyondhistory.net/coast/nature/images/shell-tools.html.

Espinosa, F. "La Pepita de Calabaza." El Poder del Consumidor, July 9, 2018. https://elpoderdelconsumidor.org/2018/07/el-poder-de-la-pepita-de-calabaza/.

FoodData Central. (n.d.). Accessed November 7, 2023. https://fdc.nal.usda.gov/fdc-app.html#/food-details/170290/nutrients.

Harvard T. H. Chan School of Public Health. "Chickpeas (Garbanzo Beans." The Nutrition Source, January 17, 2018. https://www.hsph.harvard.edu/nutritionsource/food-features/chickpeas-garbanzo-beans/.

Hester, Thomas R. "Distant Connections." n.d. Accessed March 6, 2025. https://www.texasbeyondhistory.net/st-plains/prehistory/images/distant.html.

"J. B. White Daily Life." Texas Beyond History, n.d. Accessed November 1, 2023. https://www.texasbeyondhistory.net/jbwhite/dailylife.html.

Kahn, P. H., Jr. "Children's Affiliations with Nature: Structure, Development, and the Problem of Environmental Generational Amnesia." In *Children and Nature: Psychological, Sociocultural, and Evolutionary Investigations*, edited by Peter H. Kahn and Stephen R. Kellert, 93–116. Cambridge, MA: MIT Press, 2002.

Kaika, A., and A. Racelis. "Civic Agriculture in Review: Then, Now, and Future Directions." *Journal of Agriculture, Food Systems, and Community Development* 10, no. 2 (2021): 551–72. https://doi.org/10.5304/jafscd.2021.102.030.

Keegan, M. *Southwest Indian Cookbook*. Santa Fe, NM: Clear Light Publishing, 2010.

Kraft, K. H., C. H. Brown, G. P. Nabhan, E. Luedeling, J. de J. Luna Ruiz, G. Coppens d'Eeckenbrugge, R. J. Hijmans, and P. Gepts. "Multiple Lines of Evidence for the Origin of Domesticated Chili Pepper, *Capsicum annuum*, in Mexico." *Proceedings of the National Academy of Sciences* 111, no. 17 (2014): 6165–70. https://doi.org/10.1073/pnas.1308933111.

La Vere, D. *The Texas Indians*. College Station: Texas A&M University Press, 2004.

Liber, M., I. Duarte, A. T. Maia, and H. R. Oliveira. "The History of Lentil (*Lens culinaris subsp. Culinaris*) Domestication and Spread as Revealed by Genotyping-by-Sequencing of Wild and Landrace Accessions." *Frontiers in Plant Science* 12 (2021): 628439. https://doi.org/10.3389/fpls.2021.628439.

Luis, M.-S., H.-B. Emilio, S.-M. Antonio, P.-S. Dolores, M.-P. Diana, and I. García-Montalvo. "Preliminary Study of Nicuatole, a Traditional Endemic Food Based on Zea Mays from the Central Valleys Region, Oaxaca, Mexico." *Emirates Journal of Food and Agriculture* (2023), https://doi.org/10.9755/ejfa.2023.3155.

Mahr, S. "Spinach, *Spinacia oleracea*." Wisconsin Horticulture, n.d. Accessed October 27, 2023. https://hort.extension.wisc.edu/articles/spinach-spinacia-oleracea/.

Mahr, S. "Swiss Chard." Wisconsin Horticulture, n.d. Accessed October 24, 2023. https://hort.extension.wisc.edu/articles/swiss-chard/.

Medrano, A. *Truly Texas Mexican: A Native Culinary Heritage in Recipes*. Lubbock: Texas Tech University Press, 2014.

Montaño, M. "Early Spanish Expeditions into Texas: Food Exchanges and Comida Casera." The Texas Indigenous Food Project, May 20, 2023. https://texasindigenousfood.org/chefs-lunch-showcase/.

"Nature-amaranth." Texas Beyond History, n.d. Accessed April 10, 2017. https://www.texasbeyondhistory.net/st-plains/nature/images/amaranth.html.

"Nature-prickly pear." Texas Beyond History, n.d. Accessed October 16, 2023. https://www.texasbeyondhistory.net/st-plains/nature/images/prickly.html.

"One-on-One with a Public Health Professor: Professor R. Jimenez." Video recording, August 26, 2023. https://www.youtube.com/watch?v=5HmPdvWlVCc.

Paris, H. S. "Origin and emergence of the sweet dessert watermelon, *Citrullus lanatus*." *Annals of Botany* 116, no. 2 (2015): 133–48. https://doi.org/10.1093/aob/mcv077.

Pilcher, J. M. *Planet Taco*. Oxford: Oxford University Press, 2012.

Potter, D. "Enchanted Rock." Texas Beyond History, November 2022. https://www.texasbeyondhistory.net/plateaus/images/ap16.html.

"The Prickly Meanings of the Pineapple." Biodiversity Heritage Library, January 28, 2021. https://blog.biodiversitylibrary.org/2021/01/prickly-meanings-pineapple.html.

Pu, Y.-T., Q. Luo, L.-H. Wen, Y.-R. Li, P.-H. Meng, X.-J. Wang, and G.-F. Tan. "Origin, Evolution, Breeding, and Omics of Chayote, an Important Cucurbitaceae Vegetable Crop." *Frontiers in Plant Science* 12 (2021): 739091. https://doi.org/10.3389/fpls.2021.739091.

Research and Markets. "Growth Opportunities in the $7.38 Billion Chia Seeds Market, 2033 - Includes Strategic Analysis of Key Players Glanbia, Spectrum Organic Products, Bayer, Chia Tai Seeds, The Chia Co, Mamma Chia & More." GlobeNewswire News Room, January 21, 2025. https://www.globenewswire.com/news-release/2025/01/21/3012437/28124/en/Growth-Opportunities-in-the-7-38-Billion-Chia-Seeds-Market-2033-Includes-Strategic-Analysis-of-Key-Players-Glanbia-Spectrum-Organic-Products-Bayer-Chia-Tai-Seeds-The-Chia-Co-Mamma-.html.

Sahagún, B. de. *Historia general de las cosas de la Nueva*

España I. Linkgua, 1540.
Schöndube B., O. "Los Tarascos." *Arqueología Mexicana*, August 4, 2017. https://arqueologiamexicana.mx/mexico-antiguo/los-tarascos.
Sandborn, D. "Jerusalem Artichokes: Tasty and Versatile." MSU Extension, October 31, 2016. https://www.canr.msu.edu/news/jerusalem_artichokes_tasty_and_versatile.
Secretaria de Agricultura, S. de A. y D. "Sandía, ¡fruta de colores mexicanos!" gob.mx, September 15, 2016. http://www.gob.mx/agricultura/es/articulos/sandia-fruta-de-colores-mexicanos.
Secretaria de Agricultura y Desarrollo Rural. "Xoconostle, una tuna maravillosa." Gobierno de México, n.d. Accessed November 3, 2023. http://www.gob.mx/agricultura/es/articulos/xoconostle-una-tuna-maravillosa.
Serrano, F. "Indigenous Mine Workers in the Guanajuato-Michoacán Region: Labor, Migration, and Ethnic Identity in Colonial Mexico, 1550–1800." PhD diss., UCLA, 2017. https://www.academia.edu/45032780/Indigenous_Mine_Workers_in_the_Guanajuato_Michoac%C3%A1n_Region_Labor_Migration_and_Ethnic_Identity_in_Colonial_Mexico_1550_1800.
"Sotol." Texas Beyond History, n.d. Accessed November 29, 2024. https://www.texasbeyondhistory.net/ethnobot/images/sotol.html.
Staff, A. S. N. "Protein Complementation." *American Society for Nutrition*, March 23, 2011. https://nutrition.org/protein-complementation/.
Stephens, J. M. "HS560/MV027: Beans, Willow-Leaf Lima—*Phaseolus lunatus forma salicis Van Esel*." IFAS Extension, University of Florida, October 28, 2018. https://edis.ifas.ufl.edu/publication/MV027.
"Tejas > Caddo Fundamentals > Caddo Life." Texas Beyond History, n.d. Accessed October 16, 2023. https://www.texasbeyondhistory.net/tejas/fundamentals/life.html.
Terpstra, C. "Kale: Discover the "Secret Powers" of This Superfood." Mayo Clinic Health System, March 17, 2023. https://www.mayoclinichealthsystem.org/hometown-health/speaking-of-health/the-many-types-and-health-benefits-of-kale.
Thoms, A. V. "Learning from Cabeza de Vaca." Texas Beyond History. Accessed July 9, 2024. https://www.texasbeyondhistory.net/cabeza-cooking/credits.html.
Thoms, A. V., & R. D. Mandel, eds. "Archaeological and Paleoecological Investigations at the Richard Beene Site, South-Central Texas." Center for Ecological Archaeology, Texas A&M University, 2007.
Towell, J. L. "Tecnología alimentaria prehispánica." *Estudios de Cultura Náhuatl* 39 (2008). https://nahuatl.historicas.unam.mx/index.php/ecn/article/view/15291.
UTRGV. "'Future of Food' panel Hosts Young Agriculturists." Accessed August 13, 2024. https://www.utrgv.edu/newsroom/2023/04/21/utrgv-food-summit-panel.htm.
Valdés, C. M. *La gente del mezquite: Los nómadas del noreste en la Colonia*. Biblioteca Coahuila de Derechos Humanos, 1995. https://www.mexicoescultura.com/actividad/241863/la-gente-del-mezquite-los-nomadas-del-noreste-en-la-colonia.html.
Vela, E. "Origen y domesticación de la calabaza." *Arqueología Mexicana*, October 21, 2017. http://arqueologiamexicana.mx/mexico-antiguo/origen-y-domesticacion-de-la-calabaza.
Vidal, T. M., C. A. Williams, U. D. Ramoutar, and F. Haffizulla. "Type 2 Diabetes Mellitus in Latinx Populations in the United States: A Culturally Relevant Literature Review." *Cureus* 14, no. 3 (2022). https://doi.org/10.7759/cureus.23173.
"Wild Onion." Texas Beyond History, n.d. Accessed October 28, 2023. https://www.texasbeyondhistory.net/ethnobot/images/onion.html.
Winfrey, D. H., and J. M. Day, eds. "The Indian Papers of Texas and the Southwest, 1825–1916." Texas State Historical Association, 1966. https://texashistory.unt.edu/ark:/67531/metapth786490/m2/1/high_res_d/Box2_Texas_Indian_Papers_1.pdf.
"Yaupon Tea: Nutrients, Benefits, Side Effects, and More." Healthline, June 2, 2021. https://www.healthline.com/nutrition/yaupon-tea.
Yoshida, Y. X., N. Simonsen, L. Chen, L. u. Zhang, R. Scribner, and T.-S. Tseng. "Sociodemographic Factors, Acculturation, and Nutrition Management among Hispanic American Adults with Self-reported Diabetes." *Journal of Health Care for the Poor and Underserved* 27, no. 3 (2016): 1592–607.
Zadik, B. J. *The Iberian Pig in Spain and the Americas at the time of Columbus*. Online book, 2005. https://www.bzhumdrum.com/pig/chapter4.html.
Zaragoza, M. "Cronistas documentan que las

enchiladas potosinas surgieron hasta el siglo XIX." El Sol de San Luis | Noticias Locales, Policiacas, sobre México, San Luis Potosí y el Mundo, April 14, 2022. https://www.elsoldesanluis.com.mx/local/soledad/cronistas-documentan-que-las-enchiladas-potosinas-surgieron-hasta-el-siglo-xix-8144273.html.

INDEX

acorn squash, with mole, 46
agave nectar
  in cactus and bean salad, 86
  in leeks in tomatillo salsa, 98
agroecology, 9
ajoblanco, 67
almonds
  in ajoblanco, 67
  in queso de almendras, 159
amaranth
  Indigenous uses and history, 136
  and turnips in tomatillo sauce, 136, 137
amnesia, generational, 8
apple cider vinegar
  in pickled watermelon rind and bean salad, 102
  in tomatillo salsa, 98
Arreola, Daniel D., 6
Atakapa-Ishak people, 5. *See also* Native peoples
atole, mesquite, 190
Au Gres, Michigan, 9
avocado
  in avocado and kidney bean salad, 84, 85
  in ensalada de calabacita, 92
  ensalada de calabacita y ejote, 95
  popsicle, 189

beans
  in enfrijoladas, 23
  in ensalada de calabacita y ejote, 95
  in ensalada de garbanzos y calabacitas, 96
  in garbanzo, mushroom, and red chile dip, 110
  in sopa tarasca, 82

bell pepper
  green, in bell pepper salsa, 152
  red, in avocado and kidney bean salad, 84, 85
  red, in cabbage and potato gorditas, 52, 53
  red, in eggplant tostadas, 35
  red, in mushroom paella, 148
  red, in pickled watermelon salad, 102, 103
Brenner, Leslie, 7
butter beans. *See* lima beans

cactus
  in cactus and bean salad, 86
  and cochineal beetles, 193
  history of, 6, 8, 86
  in nopal pico de gallo, 30, 156
  with red chile, 134, 135
  roasted with guajillo vinaigrette, 88, 89
  in xoconostle appetizer, 91
Caddo people
  bean farming and trading, 86
  Texas ancestors, 5
calabacita
  with achiote, 120
  calabacita salad, 92, 93
  in colache de calabacitas, 126, 127
  and garbanzo salad, 96, 97
  and garbanzo soup, 70, 71
  and green beans, 95
  in green enchiladas, 20
  indigenous origin of, 44, 92
  with mushrooms and corn, 132, 133
  in pipián verde, 44
  sautéed, 119
  sopa de calabacitas, 78
cashew crumble, 158

cashews
  in cashew cream, 164
  in cashew crumble, 158
  in mashed turnip, 138
  origin of, 158
chamoy, 155
chayote, sautéed, historical note, 123
chia
  ancestral food, 194
  pecan blueberry pudding, 194
chickpeas. *See* garbanzo beans
Chihuahua, 5
chile ancho
  in acorn squash with mole, 46
  in chile con jackfruit, 40, 41
  in enchiladas potosinas, 16, 17
  in escabeche, 160
  in garbanzo mushroom dip, 110
  in mushroom tamales, 26, 27
  in pecan and mesquite mole, 48, 49
  in pipián ranchero, 42
  in posole rojo, 74
chile con jackfruit, 40. *See also* jackfruit
chile de árbol
  in leeks and tomatillo salsa, 98
  in pipián ranchero, 42
chile guajillo
  in cactus vinaigrette, 88
  in chile sal, 161
  in garbanzo and calabacita salad, 96
  in hibiscus flower stew, 128
  in nopalitos with red chile, 134
  in sopa tarasca, 82, 83
chile jalapeño
  in kale salad, 101
  in xoconostle appetizer, 91
chile pasilla

in chile sal, 161
in garbanzo, mushroom and red chile dip, 110
in spinach enchiladas, 18
chile piquín
in hibiscus flower drowned torta, 58, 59
in watermelon and jícama salad, 105
salsa, with tomatillos and tomatoes, 168
chile poblano. *See* poblano chile
chile sal, recipe, history, 161
chile serrano
in chiles toreados, 124
in mushroom guisado, 132
in serrano crudo salsa, 169
vinaigrette, 163
chiles
domestication sites and origin, 124
with nopales, regional variations, 134
chiles toreados, 124
chili queens, 7, 8
chiltepín. *See* chile piquín
cilantro
in garbanzo and calabacita soup, 71
in nopal pico de gallo, 156
in posole verde with mushrooms, 76
in watermelon salad, 105
Coahuila, 5, 6, 26, 58, 143
Coahuiltecan
ancestors, 5, 52, 201
atole tradition, 190
exchange with Central America, 115
region, 5
Tap Pilam Coahuiltecan nation, 42, 201
cochineal beetles, 193
comida casera, 7, 30
conchitas (shell pasta), 144
cooking techniques
earth oven, 5, 42, 98
mortar, 5, 161
stone boiling, 5
corn
gelatinization, 198
green corn soup, 72
iconic ingredient, 7
in Jerusalem artichoke tart, 56
In nicuatole, 192, 193
in posole rojo, 74
in posole verde, 76
in sopa de elote, 81
in squash soup, 78
in Texas Mexican region, 30, 180, 201
with mushrooms and squash, 132, 133
corn flour, 16, 26, 28, 30, 42, 52, 62, 78, 190
corn starch, 38, 39
corn tortillas
in garbanzo dip, 110
in lentils and Swiss chard, 114
in sopa de elote, 81
in sopa tarasca, 82
cranberries
in conserve with jícama, 166
history of, 178
in rosemary cocktail, 178
Crookston, Minnesota, 9
cucurbita pepo (tatuma squash). *See* calabacita
cultural identity, 6–11. *See also* foodways
cumin
regional uses, 147
in Tex-Mex cooking, 7
in Texas Mexican trinity, 134

Dallas Morning News, 7
Des Moines, Iowa, 10
diabetes, 8, 9, 114

earth oven, 5, 42, 98
ejote. *See* green beans
enchiladas
king trumpet mushroom and squash, 20, 21
mineras, 14, 15
potosinas, 16, 17
spinach, 18, 19
enfrijoladas, 23
ensalada de calabacita y ejote, 95
entomatadas, 24
epazote
in king trumpet enchiladas, 20
in mushroom and corn dish, 132
in mushroom tacos, 36
in posole verde, 76, 77
in sopa de calabacitas, 78

farming, conventional, 201
farmworker, 9–10
filet, cauliflower, with parsley salsa, 55
food forest, 199, 201
foodways
reclaiming, 11
Texas Mexican foodways, 5, 9–11
traditional, 8, 9
See also Tex-Mex; cultural identity
frijoles. *See* beans

garbanzo beans
with calabacita salad, 96
and calabacita soup, 71
Mediterranean origin of, 96
with mushroom and red chile dip, 110
garlic
chilled garlic soup, 67
mojo de ajo, 167
roasted garlic paste, 110
in Texas Mexican trinity of spices, 147
Gault archaeological site, 6
gelatinization, 193
gorditas, 52
green beans
and calabacita salad, 95
and migrant farmwork, 9
optional ingredient in colache, 127
in pickled watermelon rind salad, 102, 103
served with mushroom and green olive rice, 147
green peas
in green corn soup, 72
in mushroom paella, 148

health disparities, 8, 9
hibiscus flower
in chile colorado, 128
hibiscus flower drowned torta, 58
origin of, 128
Hillsboro, Texas, 9
Hinds cave, archaeological evidence of cactus use, 86
hominy
in king trumpet enchiladas, 20, 21
in posole rojo, 74, 75
in posole verde, 76, 77
Huntsman, Jon, 152

jackfruit, 40. *See also* chile con jackfruit
jalapeño chile
in bell pepper salsa, 152
in kale salad, 101
pickled, in enchiladas mineras, 14, 15
pickled, as garnish, 128
toreados, 124
in tortitas de papa, 38
in xoconostles appetizer, 91
Jerusalem artichoke
in herbed corn tart, 56
history, sautéed, 131
with pipián ranchero, 42, 43
jícama
in cranberry conserve, 166
in watermelon salad, 105
in xoconostle appetizer, 91

kale
Indigenous and Mediterranean context, 101
in red jalapeño salad, 100, 101
Karankawa people, 5, 7. *See also* Native peoples

leeks
in Belgian cooking, 6
history of, 98
with tomatillo salsa, 98
and wild onion, 98
lentils
cultural history of, 113
in lentejas guisadas, 112, 113
with Swiss chard, 114
with tomato and cilantro, 113
lettuce
in enchiladas mineras, 14
in green corn soup, 72
in memelas Oaxaqueñas, 62
in pipián verde, 44
in posole verde, 76
LGBTQ+, 46
lima beans
history of, 28
with poblano rajas, 109
tamales, 28, 29
in toksel, 115

maple syrup
in chia pudding, 194
in mesquite agua fresca, 180
with quinoa pancakes, 197
in yaupon holly tea, 184
masa, 16, 26, 27, 28, 29, 30, 48, 53, 78
memelas, 62
mesquite
agua fresca, 180
atole, 190
culinary heritage, 180
flour, 30, 48, 49, 190
and pecan mole, 48, 49, 123
in traditional cooking, 5, 6, 7, 9
mesquitamal, 30
Mexican oregano
in butter beans with poblano, 109
in cactus salad vinaigrette, 86
in calabacita enchiladas, 20, 21
in calabacita salad vinaigrette, 92
in calabacitas with achiote, 120
in cauliflower filets, 55
in cebollas encurtidas, 153
in chile poblano rice, 143
in entomatadas, 24
in hibiscus flower stew, 128
in jackfruit con chile, 40
in Jerusalem artichoke tart, 56
in mushroom tacos,36
in pecan and mesquite mole, 48
in posole rojo, 74
in posole verde, 76
in sautéed chayote, 23
in xoconostles appetizer, 91
two different types, 58
migrant labor, see farmworker
mojo de ajo, 167
mole
with acorn squash, 46, 47
pecan and mezquite, 48, 49
pipián ranchero with Jerusalem artichokes, 42, 43
pipián verde with yucca and calabacitas, 44, 45
with sautéed chayote, 123
served with mesquitamal, 30, 31
Muscatine, Iowa, 10
mushrooms
in brown vegetable stock, 171
in butter beans with poblano, 109
with calabacita and corn, 132, 133
enchiladas, 20, 21
in garbanzo dip, 110
with green olive rice, 147
paella, 148, 149
in posole verde, 76,77
tacos, 36
tamales, 26
in white vegetable stock, 172

Native peoples, 5–6. *See also* Atakapa-Ishak people; Coahuiltecan; Tonkawa people
Nava, Coahuila, 8
nicuatole, 192, 193
nixtamalization, 76, 201
nopal. *See* cactus
nopalitos. *See* cactus
Nuevo Leon, 58

obesity, 8, 9, 11, 114
Olvera, Luis, 39
onion
cebollas encurtidas, 153
See also wild onion

paella, mushroom, 148, 149
paleta. *See* popsicle

pancakes, quinoa, 196, 197
pasta. *See* conchitas
pecan
archaeological evidence, 6
with chayote, sautéed, 123
in chia pudding, 194
in pecan and mesquite mole, 30, 48, 49
pemmican, 5
pepitas
Indigenous ceremonial use, 115
in mushroom and calabacita enchiladas, 20, 21
in toksel, 115
piloncillo
in atole de mesquite, 190
in chile ancho en escabeche, 160
in chile con jackfruit, 40
in kale salad, 101
in poblano and butter beans, 109
in tepache, 183
pine nuts
as garnish to complete a dish, 158
in leeks with tomatillo salsa, 98, 99
in spinach enchiladas, 18, 19
pinto beans
in cabbage potato gorditas, 52, 53
in cactus and bean salad, 86, 87
in eggplant tostadas, 35
in enfrijoladas, 23
flavor combination with corn, 52
in hibiscus torta, 58, 59
with leftover chile paste, 110
in memelas Oaxaqueñas, 62, 63
served with cactus, 134
in sopa tarasca, 82
pipián
ranchero with Jerusalem artichokes, 42, 43
related to mushroom green enchiladas, 20
verde with yucca and calabacitas, 44, 45
poblano chile
with butter beans, 109
in colache de calabacitas, 126, 127
with corn and Jerusalem artichoke tart, 56, 57
in green corn soup, 72
with mashed turnip, 138
in mushroom and calabacita enchiladas, 20, 21
in posole verde, 76, 77
in rice, 143, 144, 171
ripe version of chile ancho, 45
in sopa de elote, 81
in tamales with habas, 28, 29
pomegranate seeds, in calabacita and green bean salad, 95
popsicle, avocado, 189
posole
rojo, 74, 75
verde, 76, 77
prickly pear. *See* cactus
pumpkin seeds. *See* pepitas

quelitre. *See* amaranth
queso de almendras, 159
quinoa
history of, 197
pancakes, 196, 197

radish
accompaniment for posole rojo, 74, 75
leaves, in pipián verde, 44, 45
salsa, with zucchini cutlets, 60, 61
in tortitas de papas with salad, 38, 39
rajas de chile poblano
with butter beans, 109
in colache de calabacitas, 127
with mashed turnips, 138, 139
in tamales, 28
rice, brown
with chile poblano, 143
in chile poblano rice, 171
compared to wheat in bajicopo, 177
with green olives and mushrooms, 147
in mushroom paella, 148
Robstown, Texas, 9

saffron, 148
salads, 38, 85–102
salsa
bell pepper, 9
and butterfly garden, 5
in Mexican American dinners, 152
parsley, with cauliflower filets, 18, 19
part of traditional cooking, 38, 39
piquín, 55
piquín, with hibiscus flower torta, 56, 57
poblano, with Jerusalem artichoke tart, 58, 59
radish, with zucchini cutlets, 58, 59
ranchera, in spinach enchiladas, 60, 61
serrano crudo, 62, 63
serrano, with memelas Oaxaqueñas, 98
served with cactus and red chile, 110
served with garbanzo dip, 115
served with sautéed chayote, 123
served with toksel, 134, 135
tomatillo, with leeks, 166
tomato, with hibiscus flower torta, 168
with tortitas de papa, 169
San Antonio, Texas, 6, 7, 10, 36, 42, 58, 138, 168, 201
San Luis Potosí, 16, 58, 143
serrano chile. *See* chile serrano
shell pasta. *See* conchitas
sopa de elote (corn soup), 81
sopa tarasca, recipe, Indigenous history, 82
sotol, 5
soups, 67–82
spinach
enchiladas, 18, 19
squash
acorn, with mole, 46, 47
seeds, described by Sahagún,

115
seeds, in pipián verde, 44, 45
seeds, powdered, 76, 77
in traditional cooking, 5, 7
yellow, in mushroom enchiladas, 20, 21
See also pepitas; calabacita; zucchini
squash seeds. *See* pepitas
stock, vegetable
as a technique, 171
brown, 172
brown, in acorn squash with mole, 6
brown, in calabacita soup, 30
brown, in mesquitamal, 35
brown, in pecan mole, 44, 45
brown, in sopa Tarasca, 46, 47
white, 48, 49
white, in chile poblano rice, 72
white, in eggplant tostadas, 76, 77
white, in garbanzo dip, 78
white, in green corn soup, 81
white, in pipián verde, 82
white, in posole verde, 110
white, in sopa de elote, 143
stone boiling, 5
sunchokes. *See* Jerusalem artichokes
Swiss chard
with lentils, 114
related to spinach, 18

tamales, 26–31
Tamaulipas, 5, 44, 124
Tamōx Talōm, 199–201
Tap Pilam Coahuiltecan Nation, 42
tart, corn and Jerusalem artichoke, 56, 57
tatuma squash. *See* calabacita
tepache, 183
Texas standing committee on Indian affairs, 7
Texas Mexican oregano, 58, 143
Tex-Mex, 7, 8
toksel, 114
tomatillo
in avocado popsicle, 20, 21
in butter beans with rajas, 44, 45
in cabbage and potato gorditas, 52
in chile piquín salsa, 60
in green corn soup, 102
in Moscow markets, 109
in mushroom and calabacita enchiladas, 136
in pickled watermelon rind salad, 76, 77
in pipián verde, 98, 99
in poblano butter bean dish, 102
in posole verde, 109
in radish salsa for zucchini cutlets, 152
salsa, for leeks, 168
with turnip and amaranth, 189
Tonkawa people, 5, 7
torta, hibiscus, drowned, 58
tortitas de papa, 38
tostadas
eggplant, 35
plain, with and without oil, 32
turnip
with amaranth in tomatillo sauce, 136, 137
mashed with poblano rajas, 138, 139
Two-Spirit people, 5, 46

University of Texas Rio, Grande Valley, 8. *See also* agroecology

Vela, Luna, 30, 48, 156
vinagreta. *See* vinaigrette
vinaigrette, 71, 86, 87, 131, 163

watermelon
cultural and historical significance, 102, 105
and jícama salad, 105
pickled watermelon rind salad, 102, 103
wild onion, 98

xoconostle
in appetizer (botana), 90, 91
distinction from tuna, 91

Yanaguana, 42
yaupon holly
native ingredient, 9, 197
tea, 184
yeast
in making tepache, 183
nutritional, in cashew crumble, 158
nutritional, in queso de almendras, 159
on pineapple surface, 183
yucca
with mojo de ajo, 167
in pipián verde, 44, 45

zucchini. *See also* calabacita
with achiote, 132
in brown vegetable stock, 92
calabacita and green bean salad, 60, 61
colache de calabacitas, 126, 127
calabacita salad, 71
in calabacita soup, 95
cutlets, with radish salsa, 78
in garbanzo salad, 96
in garbanzo soup, 119
with mushrooms and corn, 171
sautéed, 120

ABOUT THE AUTHOR

Chef, food writer, and filmmaker **Adán Medrano** holds a Certificate in Culinary Arts from the Culinary Institute of America. He grew up in San Antonio, Texas, and in Northern Mexico, where he developed his expertise in the flavor profile and techniques of Indigenous Texas Mexican food. He is the author of *Truly Texas Mexican: A Native Culinary Heritage in Recipes* (TTU Press, 2014) and *Don't Count the Tortillas: The Art of Texas Mexican Cooking* (TTU Press, 2019). In his career as a foundation grant maker, he spent twenty-three years working throughout Latin America, Europe, and Asia and during his travels came to recognize the cultural importance of food.